The
Beardstown Ladies'
Pocketbook Guide
to Picking Stocks

The

Beardstown Ladies'

Pocketbook Guide

to Picking Stocks

THE BEARDSTOWN LADIES'
INVESTMENT CLUB

with Robin Dellabough

A Seth Godin Production

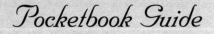

New York

We dedicate this book to Donna Strieker, Secretary of the Beardstown Chamber of Commerce, for the continuous support she has given us. Donna has shipped our books and videos all over the world, traveled to area programs with the books, and been our contact to many, many people. Donna, we thank you.

—THE BEARDSTOWN LADIES

Contents

From the Beardstown Ladies:

We acknowledge the love and support of each of our families which allows us to continue to share a portion of our lives with you, our readers.

We thank Homer G. Rieken, Broker with A. G. Edwards & Sons, who was instrumental in helping us organize our investment club, advised us to join NAIC, and continues to give enthusiastic encouragement.

We thank our employers who have supported our decision to share our knowledge with others. They have willingly given us the time away from work when needed.

We thank all the new friends that we have made across this country and abroad for their warm receptions which have reinforced our incentive to continue to share, and to say, "If we can do this, you can too!"

From Seth Godin Productions:

First and foremost, thanks to Penelope Kramer for her invaluable help in transforming the Ladies' experience and knowledge into lively prose.

Joseph Schwartz provided additional editorial and research assistance, as did Susan Kushnick, for which we are grateful.

Securities brokers Abraham Ludovici, Vice President for Investment at Dean Witter, and Richard Allman, Certified Financial Planner, generously lent their expertise in reading the manuscript to ensure its accuracy.

Our long-standing Hyperion editor, Laurie Abkemeier, has been unwavering in her support and unerring in her judgment.

Finally, thank you to Lisa DiMona, Nana Sledzieski, Sarah Silbert, Karen Watts, Ann Weinerman, and The Boss for the moral support and ginger ale throughout a long, hot summer.

Special Thanks:

We wish to thank Keith Colter and Carolyn Patterson of Central Pictures Entertainment, Inc., who created the award-winning video production "Cookin' Up Profits on Wall Street."

The Beardstown Ladies'
Investment Club

Ann Brewer, 64, secretary, charter member.

Ann Corley, 69, retired homemaker, member since 1985.

Doris Edwards, 78, elementary school principal, charter member.

Sylvia Gaushell, 86, retired art teacher, member since 1991.

Shirley Gross, 80, retired medical technologist, charter member.

Margaret Houchins, 56, former gift and flower shop owner, member since 1991.

Ruth Huston, 78, retired owner of a dry-cleaning business, charter member.

Carnell Korsmeyer, 70, hog farm owner, past president of the National Pork Board, charter member.

Hazel Lindahl, 90, retired medical technician and school nurse, charter member.

CAROL MCCOMBS, 48, insurance agent, Elsie Scheer's daughter, member since 1993.

ELSIE SCHEER, 80, retired farmer and teacher's aide, charter member.

BETTY SINNOCK, 65, bank trust officer, charter member.

MAXINE THOMAS, 76, retired bank officer, charter member.

BUFFY TILLITT-PRATT, 44, real estate broker, member since 1987.

The
Beardstown Ladies'
Pocketbook Guide
to Picking Stocks

Introduction

It still amazes us. When we wrote our first book showing how our Beardstown Ladies' Investment Club picks solid growth stocks, we never dreamed we'd become international celebrities.

We just wanted to tell folks how we formed our investment club, and to share some of the guidelines that helped us earn up to 59.5 percent on our stocks in one year. Next thing we knew, *The Beardstown Ladies' Common-Sense Investment Guide* shot to the top of the *New York Times* bestseller list, and stayed there for three months running.

Suddenly, the fourteen of us—ordinary women from a small town in west central Illinois—found ourselves jetting to New York to appear on *The Donahue Show*, cruising in limousines, visiting the New York Stock Exchange, giving advice to financial experts in London—and writing four more books.

"We're a little awestruck by it all," says Carnell Korsmeyer. "Sometimes, we stand on stage next to some prominent person and think, 'Is this really happening?' "

We think people have taken so kindly to us because we're older women. If we can learn to invest, people realize, they can too. We also fill a need for ordinary talk. So often investment books seem to be written by experts, for experts—the rest of us can't make heads or tails of them. We give common sense suggestions that everyday people can learn. We'd like to show that, as Elsie Scheer says, "You don't have to be young or rich or have a college education to learn investing. You just have to put your mind to it."

Our 90-year-old member Hazel Lindahl agrees. "We want to spread the word that you don't have to be wealthy or have connections to invest," she says. "You just have to do your homework." That's why we wrote this book expanding our investment strategies into a step-by-step guide for picking winning stocks.

At home in Beardstown (pop. 6,000), we're just ordinary people doing ordinary things—going to work, cleaning house, and doing the laundry. "Nothing has changed," says Ruth Huston, "except we're busier."

Of course, all the hoopla still excites us. It began with our first trip to *The Donahue Show* in December 1994. For some of us, this was our first airplane ride, not to mention our first trip to the Big Apple. "I liked riding in the limousine watching the people and sites of the city," says Carol McCombs. "It was just so new. It didn't seem real."

"Usually when limousines pull up to a hotel," Carnell says, "persons of renown appear. Can you imagine what people think when this bevy of ladies climb out?" More often than not, when our limo pulls up, we throw open the door and scramble out before the startled driver can get to us. We're just not accustomed to that type of service.

"I think people would be amazed at what little houses we live in," says Elsie. "We're not rich fancy people." Our members, all but four of whom are over 65, include a school principal, secretary, insurance agent, bank officer, realtor, retired businesswomen, and medical technicians, as well as homemakers and farmers. Since we follow our own rule of only buying what you need, none of us has changed our lifestyle in the last four years; the biggest news was when Sylvia Gaushell enclosed the front porch on her modest frame house. (Maybe we carry prudence a bit far. As Margaret Houchins's daughter said, "Mom, you're a Beardstown Lady. You should have a dishwasher.")

Much of our day is spent working and caring for children and grandchildren. Our free time is filled with church activities, hobbies, volunteer work— and of course, the Beardstown Ladies' Investment Club. We spent a good deal of time studying at

Shirley Gross's big dining room table, and that's where we gather to write our books: *The Beardstown Ladies' Stitch-in-Time Guide to Growing Your Nest Egg*, which helps readers plan their finances and turn their savings into a secure retirement fund, and *The Beardstown Ladies' Guide to Smart Spending for Big Savings*, which shows how to spend wisely, saving thousands of dollars on big-ticket items like houses and cars.

To visit us at home, you could fly to Chicago and drive south for four hours (though it seems like more) past cornfields and more cornfields. Turn right at Springfield and drive another hour past still more farms until you reach the intersection of Routes 100 and 125 at the edge of town.

Beardstown (named after founder Thomas Beard) is a little over a mile square. We look out over vast fields of corn, soybeans, and watermelons. In fact, we're famous for our Beardstown melons.

Driving down our quiet streets, shaded by huge soft maples and Chinese elms, you may feel you've stepped back in time. It's the kind of place where you can leave your car unlocked. We don't have a movie theater or a bookstore, but Monday night bingo always draws a big crowd. We also have 14 churches, several baseball and softball teams, and cheerleading camp in the summer.

When relatives visit, we might take them to the Elks Club for catfish or chicken fried steak. But most of the time, we go out on Route 67 to the Star

Cafe right next to Buffy Tillitt-Pratt's real estate office. No fancy decor—just red plastic glasses, Formica-topped tables, and fluorescent lights—but known for its homemade pies, and for $4.50, you get a hefty serving of roast beef, mashed potatoes, gravy, cottage cheese, and applesauce. Best of all, no matter when you arrive, you're likely to find a friend or neighbor at the next table.

Across the town square is the Chamber of Commerce which has moved from a closet-like space into a big storefront since our Beardstown books came out. There, our friend Donna Strieker helps sort our mail, answer book requests, and plan open meetings.

The club (officially known as the Beardstown Business and Professional Women's Investment Club) started in 1983, when sixteen of us decided to teach ourselves how to invest, using a combination of National Association of Investment Clubs (NAIC) guidelines and our own good sense. At that time, we hoped to make a 14.7 percent annual return to double our money in five years. We soon surpassed that, averaging more than 20 percent a year, and pulling down a stunning 59.5 percent profit in 1991.

That was the year we came to national attention. Because we'd followed NAIC's principles and used their study guides, the NAIC voted us one of their "all-star investment clubs," an unheard-of fourth year in a row. And after CBS's *This Morning* interviewed us, we were asked to do a video for the beginning investor and public television.

We put the idea to a vote at our next meeting. As we went around the circle, the answer came back: "No." "No." "No." Then our school principal, Doris Edwards, spoke up. "Well," she said, "maybe it's the teacher in me, but if we can help someone else learn, I think we should do it." She was right. The second vote was a resounding "yes." Now, whenever the speaking engagements, late-night plane rides, and airline peanuts for dinner threaten to feel like too much, we keep this goal in mind: We're helping other people become financially independent.

Especially women. Studies show that 90 percent of all American women will have to handle their own finances some day—and most have no idea how. "When I was working at the bank," says Maxine Thomas, "widows used to come in in tears. They didn't know if they had money or not. They didn't even know how to write a check."

We hope we're changing that. According to NBC financial commentator Chris Jensen, 5,000 new women's investment clubs were formed in the United States in the last three years, "many of them inspired by the Beardstown Ladies' Club." In 1960 only one in ten investment club members was a woman. Now that number is seven in ten, and all-women clubs invest almost $11 million a month.

"Ann Corley is our personal success story," says Ann Brewer. "Before she became a Beardstown Lady, she wanted her husband to handle everything. When he'd ask her to discuss finances, she absolutely refused to make any decisions on anything of importance. Luckily, he suggested she join the club in 1985. He died in 1993. Now she takes *The Wall Street Journal* and researches stocks on her own, investing in some of them even before the club does. And when she talks about her favorite stock, Intel, she just glows."

"After hearing us, many ladies feel like the stock market isn't so intimidating," Ann Corley says. "They're like me. I thought it would be too complicated. Today, I enjoy making investment decisions."

We're especially pleased that we've been able to reach young people. A number of high schools and colleges have begun using the *Beardstown Ladies' Common-Sense Investment Guide* as a classroom aid. At Illinois College in Jacksonville, a $100,000 bequest was turned over to a group of business students to invest the Beardstown way. So far, the return has surpassed their highest expectations.

Maxine says, "I guess it's the grandma in me, but it's almost become a mission to start teaching investing and saving."

This new book was born on the road. "At every appearance," says Betty Sinnock "people would come up and ask us questions we hadn't answered in the first three books: How exactly should they calculate the price/earnings ratio? Why is the upside/down ratio so important? And *how* do you fill out the stock selection guide?" They wanted more specifics about how to pick a stock. Most of all they wanted us to make it simpler to understand.

So many new investors come up to us and say, "I look at all these investment materials and wonder if I'll ever learn. Can you tell me an easier way to do it?" In this book, we want to answer all these questions in one handy package—to walk investors through the stock-picking process step by step.

Says Margaret, "The new investor is like a baby. If you say, 'Here's a steak to chew up and digest,' it's discouraging. We want to chop it into smaller bites."

We also want to share what we've learned in the last three years, and explain how the Beardstown Ladies' system has evolved. Our first investment book, *The Beardstown Ladies' Common-Sense Investment Guide*, was about how to start a club, because an investment club is such a wonderful source of support, fun, friends, and information. In this book, we focus on helping the individual investor pick winning stocks.

Investing wisely helps us build a better future for ourselves—and for the country. When we own stocks in well-run companies, we help strengthen the national economy. Beardstown has begun to extend beyond our borders, in ways we never dreamed possible. Our books have been translated into seven languages, and last Thanksgiving, we were invited to London by the National West stock brokers to encourage investment in the British stock market. We were made honorary members of ProShare (NAIC's counterpart in Great Britain).

Some experts claim we've even helped boost the American stock market. Two Czech professors drove 500 miles from a speaking engagement in Michigan to have dinner with us at the Elks Club. They had just translated our first book into Czechoslovakian, and hope it will encourage newly non-Communist Czechs to invest in their fledgling stock market—and so bolster capitalism there. In their excitement, one of them somewhat exaggerated our influence. "You're changing the global economy!" she exclaimed, tears running down her cheeks. "Were someone to ask me, would I rather meet Liz Taylor or you, I would choose you." We were almost embarrassed by the overstatement, but then we understood the tears. To her, we're an "only in America" phenomenon—ordinary people making a difference and helping other ordinary people.

As Christian women, we think the last four years have happened for a reason. Betty explains, "I think the Lord has given us the ability to do what we've done." Our willingness to share what we have learned about investing is our way of giving back.

CHAPTER ONE

How to Pick Stocks the Beardstown Ladies' Way

Let's face it. We know we should be investing and saving for our futures, but too often when we try to read—or even think—about finances, our eyes glaze over and we turn to something else. "The thing about preferred stock or stock options . . ." we read, and suddenly we remember how badly the freezer needs defrosting or the tires need to be rotated.

Why is that? We're all pretty intelligent people. We did well in school, have jobs, and raise our children. Yet when it comes to making investments, the terms and jargon make it seem so confusing that we are tempted to think we cannot invest on our own.

Nonsense. In this book, we want to prove that picking stocks is just a skill like anything else. It's like baking an apple pie. If you follow the recipe carefully, you are rewarded with flaky crust and the

11

heady aroma of hot cinnamon and apples. If you follow the recipe for stock picking, you'll wind up with a solid portfolio of investments.

If we can do it, you can too. You don't need massive amounts of money or an "in" on Wall Street. We're not rich and we're the furthest thing from Wall Street insiders. We're just the ladies next door, the women in your mother's garden club. Most of us knew nothing about stocks when we started 15 years ago. As Betty says, "I thought a portfolio was a briefcase, not the stocks you own." Some of us didn't even know how to write a check. We started out investing just $25 a month. By following the Beardstown Ladies' recipe, we've seen our investments go up as much as 59 percent in one year.

One thing we've learned is: the time to invest is now. "A few years ago," says Ann Brewer, "my son's broker told him the bubble had burst, and he sold all his stock. He probably made money, but look what he missed out on." Stocks may rise one day and drop the next, but we've discovered that over the long haul, the market goes up. "We're living in different times," says Ann. "All these baby boomers are bringing new money into the market. There's no history to tell us how long the market will rise.

"We'd like to say that there's not a person out there that can't learn and become comfortable investing," she says. "If we can do it at our ages, you can too."

But like following a recipe, you can't do it if you don't know the terms. We know a woman who has never learned to cook because she's irritated with cookbook authors. If she knew what *sauté* and *julienne* meant, she says, why on earth would she need a cookbook? Why can't they just speak English?

The same is true with finances. When some financial experts start speaking Investment-ese, they might as well be speaking a foreign language. When we don't understand, they say the same things, slower and louder, as if that would help. "*Diversify* your *portfolio*," they say. When we ask what a portfolio is, they say, "It's your *aggregate liquid securities.*"

In this book, we'll translate the simple rules of investing in the stock market into plain English. So sit back, relax, pour yourself a cup of tea, and learn with us how to cook up a rich, satisfying portfolio.

There's always been a certain aura of mystery about investing in the stock market. I think sometimes that's projected by those who are selling stocks because they want you to take their advice. Our message is: if we can do this, anybody can.
—Carnell Korsmeyer

Stocks and the Stock Market

Two phrases people throw around as if everyone knows them are "shares of stock" and "stock market." But what exactly is a share of stock?

Let's say you decide to start a little home business baking "Mama's Marvelous Pies." In no time, you're taking more orders than you can fill. You hire your sister-in-law and your cousin, quickly outgrow your kitchen, and rent a larger space. Maybe your brother contributes $20,000 to help cover new expenses, for which you promise him a fourth of the business.

One day Sam's Supermarkets calls, begging for Mama's finest—but only if you can bake and deliver 30,000 pies a day. Now you need real money fast for more cooks, ingredients, a factory, and delivery trucks. You don't have enough well-to-do brothers to cover this expense. How can you get the money? One way is to sell small pieces—or shares—of your business to anyone who will buy. Because you are selling shares in your business to anyone who comes along, this is called going public. Your company is now publicly held. If you divide the total worth of your company into 100,000 shares and someone buys 100 shares, they own 1/1000 of your company.

So what are shares of stock? The word "stock" really just means a collection of goods, like livestock or the stock on the supermarket shelves.

When you buy a share of stock, you're buying one piece of the goods. Saying we're buying stock is just a quicker way to say we're buying shares of stock.

The stock market isn't one place. We use the term loosely to refer to anything related to buying and selling stock. Sometimes we're referring to two buildings nestled in the narrow old streets of the Wall Street district where stocks are bought and sold—the New York Stock Exchange and the American Stock Exchange. (This is what we're looking at when we see pictures of brokers milling around on the floor shouting orders at each other while bells clang frantically.) Or we may be talking about the third major market, or exchange, a computerized system called Nasdaq (which stands for the National Association of Securities Dealers Automated Quotation System). Nasdaq isn't in one building. It's a sort of electronic trading post—no milling or shouting there, just a central computerized switchboard that people from all over the country dial (or e-mail) to buy and sell shares of a company.

In most cases, stocks in a given company—say Mama's Marvelous Pies—will only be sold at one of these markets, or exchanges—either on the American or the New York exchange, or on Nasdaq. It's as if you had to go to one supermarket to get Mama's Marvelous Pies, and traipse over to another one to get Papa's Perfect Pastries. Only in this case your broker's fingers do the traipsing.

Signs of Health:
The Dow Jones and Other Indexes

When we say the stock market is up or down today, we're talking about groups of selected stocks that someone has decided are important. "The New York Stock Exchange Index (or the American Stock Exchange, or Nasdaq) is down three points today," the newscaster says solemnly. She means that if you added together all the shares bought and sold on that exchange—in that market—you'd find that today, the total price of all shares in the market went down $3 per share. In other words points are the same as dollars.

When we say the Dow Jones is up, we mean the group of 30 stocks on a list—first compiled in 1884 by reporters Charles Dow and Eddie Jones who founded *The Wall Street Journal*—has on the whole done well today. If we say Standard and Poor's is down, we mean the 500 stocks that the financial publishing company tracks have lost ground.

EVERYONE'S PLAN IS DIFFERENT

I went to college during the Depression and I had to drop out in the middle and earn the money to go back. So I thought one of the nicest things I could do for my grandchildren would be to get them through college without a debt. And so far, four of them have graduated—no debt. The fifth one is my granddaughter, and she's finished her first year of school. She's a honey. She's going into architecture and study interior design, and she's a straight A student. This summer she's working for a company called Menards doing kitchen designs which is right down her line. She says it's wonderful. All these contractors come in and they give her the blueprints and she designs the cabinets they need. I said, "For heaven's sake. Stop and run one of those through a copy machine every once in a while. Someday, when you're writing a resumé, those will be excellent."

It's so important to like what you're doing in life, and not work for the paycheck. My fourth grandchild who graduated from college in forestry this year decided he wanted a master's degree because his goal in life is to run a national park.

He's going to make it. He graduated with honors and this summer he's out in Montana— here he is, working already as a ranger in a national park. And he tells me, "I get up every day and love everything I do all day. I cannot believe I'm getting paid for something I love to do." That's the gift I wanted to give him. And my stock portfolio's done it.

—Shirley Gross

The Stock Market Always Goes Up (Over Time)

Many people are afraid to invest in the stock market for two reasons: the crash of 1929 and the crash of 1987. But in spite of the drama of those sudden stock drops, the market's general direction has been up for the last 200 years. In fact, if you had bought shares in every company on the New York Stock Exchange—even the biggest losers—on any day during that time, you would have made a profit over the next 15 years, and you would have beaten bonds and savings accounts over any period exceeding 20 years—even starting in 1929. On October 19, 1987, for example, the stock market dropped 508 points to under 2,000 in one day. Just a year and a half later, it had come back. By July 1997, it was 6,200 points higher than it was before the crash. We may well be facing a downturn now. But we assume that the market will come back. It always has.

Notice that we talk about 20 *years*. This is no get-rich-quick scheme. This is a plan to grow comfortable over time. Since 1900, the 500 stocks listed on the Standard & Poor's index have moved steadily upward, making an average annual return of 9 percent, and growing an average of 11 percent a year for the last decade. This is more than twice as much as corporate bonds (4.4 percent) or Treasury bills (3.3 percent).

We want to do much better than 9 percent. Our club's goal is to buy shares in the strongest companies so our stocks grow by an average of at least 14.7 percent each year. That way we double our money every five years. In fact, over the last 15 years, we've averaged more than a 20 percent annual return (meaning for every $100 we put in that year, we got $120 back) and in 1991, we made an astounding 59 percent profit.

"After the crash of 1987, the market took about 18 months to come back," says Maxine. "Of course our investments didn't take that long because they were in such solid companies."

Bottom Line Patriotism

We believe that the stock market naturally rises over time because good companies grow and prosper, and America is filled with good companies. Businesses which soar are usually those which create unique new products, provide good service, and meet unfilled needs. In the process, they make America the world's leading economy.

Yet capitalism works only as long as growing businesses can get the money they need to expand. The major purpose of the stock market is to provide a pool of investment money for growing companies. We figure that the more money we put into well-run, innovative businesses, the better they are likely to do.

We say it's important to be an educated investor. By investing in only the best-run companies, we're casting our financial vote for good business and helping build a strong economy. That's why we agree with Louis Rukeyser who calls investing in the stock market "bottom line patriotism."

There are two kinds of investors. The first and more conservative pick a stock by looking at the fundamental value in a company, or its "fundamentals." They assume that as long as a company is well run and it keeps making more money, the value of its stock will go up. That is the type of investors we are.

Not surprisingly, fundamentalists try to buy *growth stocks*, which are shares in companies that seem likely to keep growing, because their sales are growing faster than those of the other companies in their field.

"Market timers" on the other hand, try to guess how the market is likely to behave based on the psychology of the people buying stocks and other major financial players. This is also known as "technical investing." For market timers (or "technical analysts"), the market is like an auction, where the price of a stock soars as eager beavers bid it up—often in ways that are unrelated to its real value. They try to use intuition and fancy formulas to second-guess other buyers and jump in just when a stock is about to skyrocket—and jump out just before everyone else realizes it's gotten so overpriced the price bears no relation to the company's real worth. These are the investors who make a killing in a month or a year. They're also the ones who may lose their shirts.

Some market timers assume stock prices follow the same pattern every time certain conditions prevail—falling when there's an earthquake or war, rising when interest rates drop. Others act as if the graph itself were magic, assuming that the line showing the rise and fall of stocks will repeat itself again and again in predictable patterns. (In some cases, of course, this becomes a self-fulfilling prophecy.)

We take a less risky approach, which we think guarantees that our money will grow slowly and steadily. Our job, before we buy a stock, is to look at a company carefully to make sure it is one that is likely to grow. That may sound like the old Will Rogers tag: "The way to make money in the market is to buy a stock, and when it goes up, sell it. And if it don't go up, don't buy it."

Invest What?

Many people don't think about investing, because they don't have anything to invest. Financial "planning" is limited to daydreams that a rich uncle will emerge from the woodwork, or someone will hand us a winning lottery ticket.

If you're spending your whole paycheck and more each month, you're not alone. We know how it is. When Betty Sinnock, who now serves on an advisory committee to the New York Stock Exchange, was a young wife, the only money her husband could save was the money he hid from her. Like many of us, she says, "I could always justify buying something, because it was needed for the girls, or we needed it for the house. I had not learned the discipline, which is so important, of paying yourself first, even if it's a small amount."

Since then, she's learned a few things. After paying to educate four daughters, she and her husband were at financial ground zero when she joined the first Beardstown Ladies' Club in 1980. Since then, she's accumulated a 401K pension fund and invested in more than 20 other stocks, and that doesn't include the money she's made from two investment clubs.

The hard truth is, no matter how much money we have or hope to make, we need to plan ahead.

We know a high-powered salesman whose commissions climbed to $150,000 a year by the time he was 45. He is the kind of person who would give his friends and family the shirt off his back—and then spend beyond his credit limit to buy them another. Over the years, between college tuition, lavish family vacations, and generous presents to his four children, five stepchildren, and two ex-wives, he found himself sinking into debt. Every year, instead of his savings account growing, his credit card bills got bigger. Still, when he retired at 52 with a $99,000-a-year golden parachute, he thought his pension would be plenty to see him through retirement. Unfortunately, he hadn't planned on the impact of inflation on his yearly income, which is now worth, in terms of buying power, 87 percent of what it was when he retired. He also hadn't reckoned with the cost of paying off past debts, the interest rates on his credit cards, or the fact that his children would need financial help after they left home. Just when he should be reaping the rewards of a long career, the Lexus has been traded for a Toyota, the vacations have evaporated, and he's living in a rented house. Thanks to massive long-term debt, he's struggling to get by on almost $100,000 a year.

How will the rest of us make do on less? We think it's not only possible, but easy, if you follow a few simple rules for investing and saving the Beardstown Ladies' way.

RULE #1: PAY YOURSELF FIRST

The Beardstown Ladies' First Rule of Investing is: Pay Yourself First. That's the foundation of all our savings plans. Each month, set all your bills aside until you decide how much you can pay yourself—your personal savings and investment fund. It doesn't matter whether it's $5 or $300, as long as you put something aside every month. Do the same thing with any money you get, whether it's a bonus, a tax return, or a gift from your great-aunt. The second it arrives in your mailbox, set part of it aside to invest for your future.

This is so important because, as many of us have noticed, the only way to get ahead these days is if your money is earning money. We don't have time to earn enough for financial security ourselves. Our money has to be working for us.

That's why we need to find that first $1,000, or even $100, to start the money growing. As Ann Brewer says, "The most important thing is to simply learn to start saving and investing. A lot of people at the end of the month, before they get their paychecks, are broke."

Do you think paying yourself first means your lights will be turned off or you'll be skipping dinner this month? If so, take a closer look at your finances.

How to find hidden money in your budget: You can't get blood from a turnip, but you can squeeze extra money out of your income three ways.

1. Spend smart. Be a smart shopper. Invest your time and energy in saving thousands of dollars on big-ticket items like your home and your car. Having lower mortgage or car payments is like having a few hundred extra dollars each month in your pay envelope. This will do you a lot more good than clipping coupons or driving out of your way to save a few cents on dish soap (though that can't hurt either). In *The Beardstown Ladies' Guide to Smart Spending for Big Savings* we explained our tricks for saving money on cars, houses, appliances, insurance, children's education, and other major expenditures.

One couple we know bought their car for $3,000 less than the sticker price because it had been driven 150 miles and was considered used. Another friend of ours saved thousands of dollars on her first home by persuading her landlord to sell her the house she was renting without putting it on the market—thus saving the realtor's fees.

Changing the way you buy the big things can dramatically change your standard of living. Often a few hours of negotiation or research can save you thousands of dollars. Consider it a second job—it's pretty well paid.

2. Know what you really want. "You need to think about exactly what it is you are buying," says Carnell. "If you focus on buying a car, then perhaps all the extras will look very attractive. But if you remember that you're buying transportation that meets your particular needs, it's easier to see which of the niceties you can do without."

A young Los Angeles couple was looking for a home in a particular suburb because it had good schools. When they found a house that met their needs, they were stunned by its $600,000 price tag and $12,000 property taxes. Realizing they wanted education and shelter, not that particular suburb, they bought a house three miles away at half the price, saving themselves $20,000 every year. Half of the savings they spent on sending their son to a

Catholic school. The rest they invested to finance four years of college at the best engineering school in the country. Basically, they bought themselves a good private education, with college thrown in for free.

3. Small savings do add up. If you're not buying a car, home, or washing machine (a friend of ours bought a used machine for $150 ten years ago—not glamorous to look at but it still works great!), you can still find extra money in your budget by reconsidering your priorities. If you want to have fun with your family, how about replacing an expensive dinner out with a picnic in the park? Or exchanging one night a month at the movies ($25 for two with popcorn and drink) for a video and homemade snacks ($3.95), and putting the extra $21.05 aside. It will add up.

RULE #2: DO YOUR HOMEWORK

"The question people ask most often," Doris says, "is do we have a hot tip for them. We do. Our hot tip is, 'do your homework.'"

Amen. The success of the Beardstown Ladies' method of picking stocks depends on doing our homework and being selective. We can't stress this enough. You simply cannot make good investment decisions on the spur of the moment, based on intuition or that hot tip you got at the beauty parlor. You need to have the patience to study each stock before you buy it. As with a good recipe, you need to make sure all the ingredients are right and follow the instructions step by step before you put your money in the market and hope your profits will rise.

Easy to say, but where do we start? Picking a stock the Beardstown Ladies' way is a simple process of elimination, like rounds in a sports tournament. We start with a number of stocks in the same industry that look good, put them through some tests, and keep sifting out the weaker ones until we've found the one stock that looks the best. Then we go back, look at that stock again, using our common sense, and make a final decision. If it turns out it's not really good enough to buy, we go back to the drawing board.

But how do we decide which stocks to study? Well, we have a four-step process we use with every stock we investigate. Although we'll describe each step in more depth later in the book, here's a brief summary:

Step one: pick an industry. The first step is to pick an industry we think is on the upswing. The barrel hoop industry would have been a good choice in the 1820s; hula hoops were hot in the 1950s; at the moment, pharmaceuticals and fast food are on a roll. Let's say we're interested in fast foods. We stroll down to the library and pull a thick, glossy book off the shelf called the *Value Line Investment Survey*. Turning to a section marked "Timely

Stocks in Timely Industries," we find that restaurants are doing well. We decide to look into fast food restaurants.

There are several investment guides like *Value Line* written by experts on business and the stock market. "*Value Line* is our investment Bible," Ruth says. We rely on it because it has almost everything we could want to know about a given company crammed into one densely written page (see Figure 1–1 on pages 30–1).

Step two: narrow the field. Having chosen the fast food industry, we decide to investigate McDonald's, Wendy's, and Boston Chicken. We test these three stocks by looking up the four or five most important numbers about them on their page in *Value Line*. We check the most significant ratings first, so we don't waste time going through the whole stock selection process for a stock that would have been knocked out of the running at the beginning.

To us, the first thing to look at is the company's financial strength. *Value Line* rates a company from A + + to C. If a company has a C rating, there's no point in wasting any more time studying it. That may seem obvious, but you'd be surprised how many people skip over this common sense rule.

This financial strength rating predicts how solid a company is and how well it is likely to do, based largely on its earnings, debt, and past performance. We have a friend who says when he's hiring someone, he really wants to see just one thing—his elementary school attendance record. We know what he means. What someone has done in the past is a pretty good guide to what they'll do in the future. We think the same is true of a company, which is why we look at their history to predict what they're going to do next. (Of course, that changes if all their managers are fired. If that happens, we can check out the way the company's new CEO ran his last company.)

If the financial strength rating is good, we look next at two *Value Line* ratings: the stock's timeliness, (how likely it is that the price will rise in the next 12 months), and its safety (whether the stock is a safe buy in a company that's likely to remain financially strong.

Then we look at the debt—how much money the company owes—and the beta, which shows whether the price will rise or fall faster than the market.

Finally we look at the price/earnings ratio history, which shows whether the stock's price is too high for the amount of money the company is likely to earn.

Step three: fill out the Stock Selection Guide. Let's say McDonald's has scored a home run in all these categories. Then it's worth it to us to fill out a worksheet called the Stock Selection Guide—a test for stocks, not unlike those magazine tests you take to find out if you and your spouse are compati-

COCA-COLA NYSE-KO | **RECENT PRICE** 68 | **PE RATIO** 40.0 (Trailing: 43.9 Median: 21.0) | **RELATIVE PE RATIO** 2.22 | **DIV'D YLD** 0.9% | **VALUE LINE**

TIMELINESS 2 (Relative Price Perform Next 12 Mos.) — Above Average

SAFETY 1 Highest
(Scale: 1 Highest to 5 Lowest)

BETA 1.15 (1.00 = Market)

2000-02 PROJECTIONS
	Price	Gain	Ann'l Total Return
High	89	(+35%)	8%
Low	68	(+5%)	Nil

Options: CBOE

● VALUE LINE PUB., INC. 00-02

	1981	1982	1983	1984	1985	1986	1987	1988	1989	1990	1991	1992	1993	1994	1995	1996	1997	1998	© VALUE LINE PUB., INC.	00-02
Sales per sh A	1.98	1.92	2.09	2.35	2.56	2.81	2.57	2.94	3.33	3.83	4.35	5.00	5.36	6.34	7.19	7.48	7.90	8.90	Sales per sh A	12.60
"Cash Flow" per sh	.20	.22	.22	.25	.28	.31	.36	.43	.50	.61	.71	.84	.98	1.16	1.37	1.60	1.90	2.20	"Cash Flow" per sh	3.15
Earnings per sh B	.15	.16	.17	.20	.20	.28	.36	.36	.42	.51	.61	.72	.84	.99	1.19	1.40	1.70	1.95	Earnings per sh B	2.85
Div'ds Decl'd per sh C	.10	.10	.11	.11	.12	.13	.14	.15	.17	.20	.24	.28	.34	.39	.44	.50	.56	.62	Div'ds Decl'd per sh C	.86
Cap'l Spending per sh	.10	.10	.11	.11	.16	.12	.14	.17	.17	.22	.30	.41	.31	.34	.37	.40	.45	.50	Cap'l Spending per sh	.65
Book Value per sh D	.77	.85	.89	.88	.96	1.14	1.08	1.07	1.18	1.41	1.67	1.49	1.77	2.05	2.48	2.48	3.10	3.80	Book Value per sh D	6.50

FIGURE 1-1

CURRENT POSITION	1995	1996	3/31/97
Cash Assets	1315.0	1658.0	2237.0
Receivables	1695.0	1641.0	1697.0
Inventory (Avg Cst)	1117.0	952.0	1051.0
Other	1048.0	959.0	1005.0
Current Assets	5450.0	5969.0	6340.0
Accts Payable	2894.0	2972.0	3104.0
Debt Due	2923.0	3397.0	2839.0
Other	1531.0	1037.0	1367.0
Current Liab.	7348.0	7406.0	7310.0

ANNUAL RATES of change (per sh)	Past 10 Yrs.	Past 5 Yrs.	Est'd '94-'96 to '00-'02
Sales	10.5%	13.0%	10.5%
"Cash Flow"	17.0%	18.0%	15.0%
Earnings	18.0%	18.5%	15.5%
Dividends	13.5%	17.0%	12.0%
Book Value	8.5%	9.5%	10.5%

QUARTERLY SALES ($ mill) Cal-endar	Mar.31	Jun.30	Sep.30	Dec.31	Full Year
1994	3352	4342	4461	4017	16172
1995	3854	4936	4895	4333	18018
1996	4194	4853	4956	4343	18546
1997	4138	5075	5150	4962	19325
1998	4525	5800	5625	5450	21400

EARNINGS PER SHARE B Cal-endar	Mar.31	Jun.30	Sep.30	Dec.31	Full Year
1994	.20	.30	.28	.21	.99
1995	.25	.36	.32	.26	1.19
1996	.28	.42	.39	.31	1.40
1997	.40	.53	.43	.34	1.70
1998	.45	.58	.50	.42	1.95

QUARTERLY DIVIDENDS PAID C = Cal-endar	Mar.31	Jun.30	Sep.30	Dec.31	Full Year
1993	–	.085	.085	.17	.34
1994	–	.098	.098	.195	.39
1995	–	.11	.11	.22	.44
1996	–	.125	.125	.25	.50
1997	–	.14	.14		

(A) Includes Columbia Pictures: 7/82-12/86. (B) Based on average shares outstanding thru late Oct. Excludes special gains: '81, 2¢; '86, 8¢; disc. op. gains (loss) '83, (1¢); '85, 2¢; '89, 2¢; nonrec. gain (loss) '89, 53¢; '92, (2¢). (C) Next div'd meeting about Oct. 16. Goes ex Sept. 11. Div'd paid about Oct. 1, July 1, Oct. 1, Dec. 15. Next earnings report due late Oct. (D) Div'd reinvestment plan avail. (D) Incl. intangibles. In '96: $753.2 mill., 30¢/sh. (E) In millions, adj. for stock splits.

BUSINESS: The Coca-Cola Company is the world's largest soft drink company. Distributes major brands (Coca-Cola, Sprite, Fanta, TAB, etc.) through bottlers throughout the world. Foreign (non-U.S.) operations accounted for 67% of net sales and 79% of profits in 1996. Food division, sold 1/3's and distribution of juice products (Minute Maid, Five Alive, Hi-C, etc.). Coca-Cola Enterprises, 45%-owned soft drink bottler. Advertising costs, 7.7% of sales. Has approximately 26,000 employees; 225,000 stockholders. Berkshire Hathaway owns 8.1% of stock (1997 Proxy). 1996 dep. rate: 8.5%. Estimated plant age: 4 years. Chairman and Chief Executive Officer: Roberto C. Goizueta. Incorporated: Delaware. Address: One Coca-Cola Plaza, Atlanta, Georgia 30313. Tel.: 404-676-2121.

Coca-Cola's earnings moved sharply again in first half of 1997, although sales actually fell. The decline in the top line was the result of the sale in 1996 of previously consolidated bottling operations in France, Belgium, and east Germany and a stronger U.S. dollar. Worldwide gallon shipments of concentrates were up 8% for the six months, and there were selective price increases. Profit margins improved as concentrate sales accounted for a larger portion of the business, and there were sizable gains ($0.16 a share after taxes) from the sale of bottlers in the United Kingdom and the Philippines. (Coca-Cola has a long-term strategy of taking equity positions in bottlers that need capital and then sometime later usually selling those positions when a bottler gets stronger; since this is done on a regular basis, the company considers any gains to be part of normal operating income, and we have treated it the same way.) With fewer shares outstanding, share earnings were up 31%.

Revenues and profit growth should be strong for the rest of this year and in 1998, although the increase next year will probably be somewhat less than in this year since capital gains are likely to be smaller. In the U.S., the core brands are all doing well, and we expect that to continue. Two new products, Surge and Citra look promising, and Barq's, Powerade, Fruitopia, and Nestea should have higher sales. Rapid growth is expected again overseas, where Coke is the dominant soft drink brand in most markets. Demand has been increasing particularly fast in East Central Europe, China, India, and, recently, the Middle East.

The company's goal is to increase profits 15%-20% a year, and we think it will be successful in doing that in the coming 3 to 5 years. Worldwide demand for soft drinks will continue to grow, and Coke has the infrastructure, financial strength, and marketing skills to take advantage of it.

Coke shares continue to be ranked to outperform the market in the coming six to 12 months, but because the price has risen so much and the price/earnings ratio is so high, we look for only modest appreciation, at best, out 3 to 5 years.
Stephen Sanborn, CFA   August 15, 1997

Company's Financial Strength	A++
Stock's Price Stability	85
Price Growth Persistence	80
Earnings Predictability	100

To subscribe call 1-800-833-0046.

ble. You know the type: "Answer ten questions, add up the score, and you'll see whether you're deliriously happy or headed for divorce." Only the Stock Selection Guide, created by the National Association of Investment Clubs, is more profitable. It takes a little time, patience, and some junior high math, but if you're willing to spend two or more hours at your desk with a sharpened Ticonderoga, you may make yourself thousands of dollars.

As Carol says, "The Stock Selection Guide is the meat and potatoes of the Beardstown method."

Buffy can't understand why anyone wouldn't be eager to fill out the worksheet. "The more tools you use, the more you reduce your risk," she says. "Anybody can buy a stock they like just because they like it. If they have the money, I guess that's fine. The odds are better than buying a lottery ticket. But as with anything, the more information you have, the better your odds. You're equipped to make a better decision."

Sylvia adds, "Some people fear they'll lose their savings if they invest in stocks. But they don't have to. If they do the stock selection guide, it tells them thoroughly in black and white whether a stock is in the buy range, whether they would best continue to look at it—or whether they don't want to be bothered with it at all."

Step 4: Follow that stock! Once we finally decide a stock is worth buying, we expect to hold on to it for a long, long time. But that doesn't mean our job is over when the order is placed. "We buy stocks to hold," says Hazel, "not to forget." That means that every month, we reexamine each stock we own to make sure it's still worth keeping. We find this out by reading the annual report (which is sent to all stockholders), *The Wall Street Journal*, other financial publications, and reviewing the stock's numbers in *Value Line*, which is updated quarterly.

RULE #3: INVEST IN DIFFERENT AREAS

The Beardstown Ladies' method is very effective. That doesn't mean that it's magic or that we pick nothing but winners. We think of the "Rule of Five." As Ann Corley says, of any five stocks we pick, "one will probably be a blockbuster, one may be a loser, and three will probably do as we expected. Even averaging in the loser, we make a good profit that way."

One way to guarantee that is to buy stocks in a number of different industries—say electronics, tires, and soft drinks. That way, if the whole electronics industry starts to go under, taking our stocks with it, we're covered. When you diversify— buy stock in a number of diverse (different) industries—you spread out your risk, as well as raise your chances of striking paydirt.

Spreading the risk further: The risk/reward trade-off. The general rule of thumb for investments is: the higher the risk, the higher the potential reward. Stocks are considered a relatively high risk/high return investment. You can make a huge return each year, but you can also lose everything. With a low-risk, low return investment, like an interest-bearing savings account or treasury bills, you make less money, but what you do make is guaranteed. We like investing in growth stocks because we think that by doing your homework, you can minimize the risk while maximizing the reward. Even so, most of us have part of our money invested in low-risk investments as well.

NAIC Guidelines

We'd like to gratefully acknowledge that much of the Beardstown Ladies' method is inspired by investment guidelines put out by the National Association of Investment Clubs. They are:

1. *Invest a set sum in common stocks once a month, regardless of market conditions.*

2. *Reinvest dividends and capital gains immediately.*

3. *Buy growth stocks—companies whose sales are increasing at a rate faster than their industry in general, and that seem likely to keep growing.*

4. *Diversify in different sizes of companies and in industries.*

RULE #4: INVEST THE SAME AMOUNT
EVERY MONTH

Making it a rule to invest the same amount every month is like a forced savings plan: it gently steers us towards taking advantage of the magic of compound earnings in spite of ourselves. But how do compound earnings work?

Let's say you buy 100 shares of stock in Mama's Marvelous Pies for $10 apiece. In the next year, Mama's, like many companies, pays you a tiny percent of its profits—let's say 30 cents a share—for each share you own. This payment is called a dividend (part of the profits divided among the shareholders).

Now it's a year later. Mama's stock has gone up to $15 a share, and you've also made $30 in dividends. That's like free money. You take that money and use it to buy two more shares of Mama's (at $15). If all goes well, not only will the value of the two "free" shares you bought go up, but the extra shares will pay you that much more in dividends, which you can then use to buy even more stock.

Investing the same amount every month also forces us to buy more shares when prices are low. If you put in $100 when a given stock is $10 apiece, you'll get 10 shares for your money. If the price drops to $5 and you force yourself to keep buying (because your research shows this is still a good buy), you get 20 shares, but because of a system called dollar-cost averaging (which we'll explain in

Chapter Eight), you end up making more over time.

Most important, investing the same amount of money forces us to keep buying stock when the market goes down. Which brings us to—

RULE #5: WHEN THE MARKET DROPS, GO SHOPPING!

When the Dow Jones average is plummeting and the experts tell us the bubble has burst, all you want to do is turn tail and run. That's human nature. But that's exactly when experienced, successful investors get right in there, and buy, buy, buy. History has shown that dips which seem disastrous do end—in time—and since we don't try to time the market, we can wait them out.

For example, after the Dow Jones fell 508 points on October 19, 1987, "we bought as many stocks as we could before prices started to go up again," recalls Betty Sinnock. "We wished we had more money to invest because there were so many stocks we were anxious to buy." At that point, our investments were worth $24,598. By November 7, their value had dropped to $17,326, a 28.7 percent loss in one month, but we didn't panic. Instead we bought 25 shares of investment company A. G. Edwards and 40 shares of Rollins, a company specializing in lawn care and home security. We were so anxious to take advantage of their bargain prices, we voted to pay our December dues early so we could buy the shares.

Our eagerness paid off. When all was said and done, we had reaped a 79 percent gain by the time A. G. Edwards closed at the end of December 1993. Rollins did even better, with gains of 84 percent. By 1997, A. G. Edwards had gone up to 40. (We sold Rollins at a profit in 1996.)

Margaret says that buying stocks when no one else is buying is like hitting the January Christmas sales—you're getting the same merchandise for a much lower price. Waiting for the market to rise again before venturing to buy is like waiting for the sale to be over before walking into a department store. Over the years we've learned that when the going gets tough, the tough go shopping—and make money doing it.

Well, after promising not to shower you with jargon, we ended up throwing lots of new words at you after all. But you've come through with flying colors, and are well on your way to becoming an informed, successful investor. As we told you, investing can be simple. We're not saying there's no risk. There is. We're just saying if you do your homework and hold stock in solid companies over the long term, your chances of making a profit are extremely good.

CHAPTER TWO

The Process of Elimination

It always surprises us that when people talk about picking stocks, almost no one mentions how much fun it is. Reading *The Wall Street Journal* or *Value Line* is like reading a combination cliffhanger, mystery, and sports story—on every page, there are thrilling triumphs, crushing defeats, sudden upsets, or comeback stories—along with clues as to how they will all turn out. And if you can follow the clues and guess the ending, you will be rewarded. Not many hobbies can make that claim.

You also get the real scoop on the nation's corporate giants—the unvarnished truth about the companies we deal with every day. You can find out what's happening behind the scenes at Nike, or what went wrong at Apple, in surprisingly frank terms. Browsing through *Value Line* you might notice that the new fast food chain you thought was booming is only a C-rated company, or the computer firm you thought was on the ropes is bouncing back. Why? They tell you right there, in an easy-to-read 400-word report.

A friend of ours, who's perfectly solvent but so leary of anything financial she avoids looking at her bills, has gotten hooked on investing. She's not alone. "I love reading *Value Line*," says Ann Brewer. "It's addictive. You look at the page on Hershey's and think, 'I thought they just made cocoa and candy. Who knew they made all these pastas and things?' It makes you want to turn the page and find out about the next company."

Elsie agrees. "It's fun studying all the different companies," she says. "It's amazing how diversified some of them really are—all the different things they make. Like Sara Lee. Who would think they manufactured hosiery? And I had no idea that Pepsi owned Taco Bell and Kentucky Fried Chicken."

Value Line, which looks about as inviting as a railroad time table, turns out to be a real page-turner. Reading it, you might even forget that the point of all the browsing is to pick a stock. But we haven't. It's time to get started.

Where Do I Start?

We know a teacher who gives her students a foolproof trick for taking any test, from a pop quiz to the SATs: First, she says, breeze through the whole test quickly, answering just the easy questions, the ones you can do in a snap. That way, you won't leave sure things unanswered by wasting too much time on one brain-teaser. You'll at least pass the test. After nailing the easy ones, you then go back and work out the more time-consuming problems, raising your C+ to an A.

We use the same system choosing stocks. We start by answering the simple questions—most of which *Value Line* answers for us. If this first round of answers shows our company has promise, we tackle the harder questions, to ensure the stock we finally choose rates an A+. This is the "easy question" chapter.

We need to remember that all the numbers and ratings are just ways to answer one question: Is this company a solid, well-run, forward-thinking business that will keep growing over the years?

"The key is that when you're buying stock," Buffy says, "you're buying a little part of the company. You don't want to buy it because it might be popular. You don't want the next fad. You want a company that's making money, that will continue to make more money until their money makes money. Even if you're just buying 100 shares, you need to act as if you were buying the company—because you are. You have to look at it as if you were investing your hard-earned dollars to be a partner in that business, because that's what you're doing."

If you were the brother of Mama, founder of Mama's Marvelous Pies, and you knew she couldn't cook, or couldn't handle finances, or had a little gambling problem, you probably wouldn't invest in her business, no matter how much you loved her. You'd only sink your life savings into Mama's if you knew she baked flaky crusts and had a way with a dollar. Since you don't have that kind of firsthand knowledge about most businesses, you have to look up the facts in an investment guide like *Value Line* or Standard and Poor's. As we've said before, we find *Value Line* the easiest to use.

Choosing an Industry: Semiconductors or Soft Drinks?

Look up what? Since this is a process of elimination, we start by picking out the growth industry we want to invest in—computers, soft drinks, fast foods. We're looking for an industry which is timely, meaning it's on the upswing, coming into its own—one producing a medical breakthrough or a better mousetrap—not something obsolete like typewriters or dial phones. Timeliness measures how hot the industry or business is right now—how well it will do in the next six months to a year.

When a Wal-Mart opened in Beardstown, we noticed the parking lot was always full, shoppers' carts were always loaded, and the checkout clerks were always busy. That sparked our interest, so we looked it up in *Value Line* and sure enough, the retail industry as a whole was doing very well, and Wal-Mart was doing even better. We liked what we saw and ended up investing.

To find out whether an industry is timely, we look it up in *Value Line*'s 100 "Industries, in Order of Timeliness" in the Index of the publication. For example, in July 1997, coal/alternative energy was the most timely industry, cosmetics was fourth, computers fifth, soft drinks nineteenth, and gold and silver mining eighty-ninth. The folks at *Value Line* figure out the timeliness of an industry by taking the average timeliness of all the stocks in that industry.

"When we decide what industry to look at," says Margaret, "we use common sense and think about the economy. For example, you know how expensive prescriptions are. You know everybody needs health care, and you know the population is getting older. It just makes sense that pharmaceuticals or medical care would be an excellent field right now." Sure enough, medical services ranks sixth on the *Value Line* list.

As a farmer and former member of the National Pork Board, Carnell has kept her eye on developments in the fast food industry. Like many of us, she has noticed the trend toward "home style" fast food, bought in stores but served around the kitchen table. "The food industry is changing because the consumer has changed," she says. "The consumer still wants things that can be prepared in a hurry, but if they buy it in the grocery store and take it home, they can get away from eating in fast food places. They have more sense of eating in, eating at home."

We've always liked investing in industries whose products or services we use—things we know personally. But we also want to make sure we have a broad range of stocks so we don't have all our eggs in one basket. "We come from a small town and are somewhat alike in our makeup and backgrounds," says Carnell. "If we only select those things we know and understand, pretty soon our portfolio won't be very diversified."

That's why these days, we sometimes reverse the process—looking at unfamiliar industries in *Value Line*, picking out one which is timely, and then learning more about it.

Of course, as Buffy says, the industry rank is fickle. An industry which is number four on the list one month can be fourteen the next with no change in the quality of the stocks. If two toy companies come out with popular new computer games at Christmas, they may boost the average rank of the whole industry for December. Toys would climb a few notches, pushing other industries down briefly, without really changing anything important about the stocks. Since we're buying our stock for the long haul, we don't worry whether our industry is the most timely. We just like to know it's consistently one of the top 35.

How to Choose Your Stock: The Right Ingredients
Once you find an industry to investigate, you're ready for step two: researching stocks. We try to compare three stocks in the same industry. Otherwise, as Hazel says, we'd be comparing apples and oranges. In this chapter, we'll start with three fast food restaurants: McDonald's, Boston Chicken (now Boston Market), and Wendy's. (Remember, *don't* run out and buy the best-looking stock at the end of the next chapter. Any numbers we look at here only apply to stocks bought on or near June 20, 1997—the day our sample *Value Line* pages were published. Things have changed since then. This is just an exercise to warm up your stock-picking muscles.)

There's a reason this is the easy chapter. Almost everything in the world you could want to know for this research is crammed into one tightly written page in *Value Line*. We're just looking it up. (See Figures 2-1, 2-2, and 2-3, pages 46–51.)

But what do we want to know first? Which of our top ten ingredients is most important? It doesn't really matter. As Sylvia says, "They wouldn't be there if they weren't all important." Which one carries the most weight with you depends on what you care about.

Maxine looks first at the timeliness, safety, and

beta rankings at the upper left side of the page; Carnell's eye goes straight to financial strength in the lower right-hand corner. Ann Corley glances first at debt and Ruth and Buffy check sales and earnings. The truth is, all these ingredients have to be right for a stock to stay in the running.

Some riskier stocks tempt us with quick profits; others promise safety in return for slower growth. "In that case, it's risk versus comfort level," says Carnell. "Which ingredient you look at first or weigh most heavily will vary by individual. Their financial plan varies, so their criteria may too."

"You want to know what they're doing, what they're producing," says Ann Brewer. "Then you look in *Value Line* and see their timeliness and safety, how much debt they have, how well they're managed, and how much they're earning. But in the end what they're doing is the most important thing."

So, now let's look at our three sample companies in detail.

1. Financial strength (From A + + to C, on lower right-hand corner of the page.) This rating reflects how much money the company is making, how high their debts are, and whether *Value Line* analysts think they're well managed.

The relative ratings range from strongest down to weakest in nine steps:

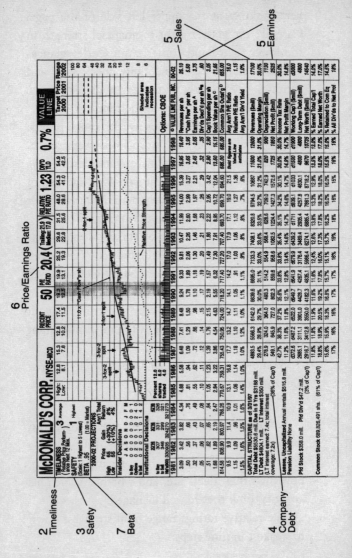

FIGURE 2-1

CURRENT POSITION	1995	1996	3/31/1997
Cash Assets	334.8	329.9	299.8
Receivables	373.0	—	—
Inventory (FIFO)	58.0	69.8	60.4
Other	185.7	235.9	220.9
Current Assets	955.8	1102.5	1010.1
Accts Payable	564.3	638.0	178.5
Debt Due	577.2	—	726.5
Other	652.4	804.0	834.8
Current Liab.	1794.9	2185.3	2039.8

ANNUAL RATES of change (per sh)	Past 10 Yrs.	Past 5 Yrs.	Est'd '94-'96 to '00-'02
Revenues	11.0%	9.0%	11.0%
"Cash Flow"	13.5%	12.5%	11.5%
Earnings	13.5%	12.5%	11.5%
Dividends	10.5%	9.0%	5.0%
Book Value	14.0%	14.0%	12.5%

Cal-endar	QUARTERLY REVENUES ($ mill.) Mar.31	Jun.30	Sep.30	Dec.31	Full Year
1994	1796	2029	2225	2270	8320.6
1995	2161	2467	2750	2385	9794.5
1996	2425	2665	2855	3107	11007
1997	2618	2875	3000	3107	11600
1998	2850	3125	3250	3375	12600

Cal-endar	EARNINGS PER SHARE A Mar.31	Jun.30	Sep.30	Dec.31	Full Year
1994	.33	.44	.48	.43	1.68
1995	.39	.56	.59	.58	1.97
1996	.42	.59	.62	.63	2.21
1997	.49	.69	.70	.69	2.45
1998	.53	.68	.75	.69	2.65

Cal-endar	QUARTERLY DIVIDENDS PAID B ■ Mar.31	Jun.30	Sep.30	Dec.31	Full Year
1993	.05	.054	.054	.053	.21
1994	.054	.06	.06	.06	.23
1995	.06	.067	.067	.067	.26
1996	.067	.075	.075	.075	.29
1997	.075	.0825			

(A) Based on average shares outstanding. Includes intangibles. In '96: $747 mill., adjusted for stock splits. Next earnings report due late July.

(B) Next dividend meeting about July 16. Goes ex-dividend about Aug 24. Approximate dividend payment dates: Mar 14, June 15, September 13, and December 13. Dividend reinvestment plan available.

BUSINESS: McDonald's Corp. licenses and operates a chain of 21,022 fast-food restaurants throughout the U.S., Canada, and overseas under the name of "McDonald's". About 63% of units are operated by franchisees; 21% by company; 16% by affiliates. About 42% of units are foreign. Foreign operations (in 101 countries) provide about 49% of systemwide sales; 37% of pretax profits. Company does not sell equipment, food, or supplies to franchisees. 1996 depreciation rate: 3.9%. Has 237,000 employees, 925,000 shareholders. Directors and officers control about 1.1% of common (497 Proxy). Chairman and Chief Executive Officer: Michael R. Quinlan. Incorporated: DE. Address: 1 McDonald's Plaza, Oak Brook, Illinois 60521. Telephone: 630-623-7428.

We believe investors will eventually look back on the present as a watershed period for McDonald's, the company that invented fast food on a mass scale and pioneered such widely known products as the Big Mac and chicken nuggets. In the international arena, the company has some sluggish periods (such as last April) and some better periods (probably May). But, on balance, there is still lots of opportunity to grow overseas, and that's where most of MCD's expansion is likely to take place in the years ahead. But the U.S. market continues to dominate Wall Street's perception of MCD and the news here hasn't been so good. Comparable unit sales comparisons (ex special promotions such as the recent one involving Beanie Babies) have often been down. And in a commendable quest for convenience company-owned units wind up competing against franchisees; a situation that may be tolerable when business is brisk but becomes infuriating when "comps" are poor. More basically, MCD stumbled in areas in which it really needs to shine. The latest value message fizzled. Being a price/value leader has long been a part of this company's strategy. But a recent $0.55 promotion failed to generate interest in the Big Mac (confusion regarding requirements for purchase of drinks and fries didn't help) and is now being limited to breakfast. What's worse, people now are so attuned to menu cutting, we wonder if MCD can ever make decent money from its core Big Mac brand.

A taste initiative is falling short. The Deluxe line introduced in '96 to appeal to adult tastes hasn't generated much incremental business for the company.

Marketing messages aren't getting through. Besides ill-starred campaigns involving the Deluxe line and the $0.55 burgers, we're not sure the ongoing "My McDonald's" campaign is succeeding.

Franchisees are restless. They rejected a program that would guarantee meal delivery within a specified time.

But this neutrally ranked stock may be an interesting special situation. We doubt there's much room for bad news. But there's plenty of room for favorable surprises, particularly of the sort resulting from a bolder strategic retreat.

Marc H. Gerstein   June 20, 1997

8 Management

1 Financial Strength

Company's Financial Strength	A+
Stock's Price Stability	90
Price Growth Persistence	100
Earnings Predictability	100

To subscribe call 1-800-833-0046

BOSTON CHICKEN NDQ-BOST | RECENT PRICE 16 | P/E RATIO 12.8 (Trailing 14.7 Median: NMF) | RELATIVE P/E RATIO 0.77 | DIV'D YLD Nil | VALUE LINE

TIMELINESS 3 Average (Relative Price Perform. Next 12 Mos.)
SAFETY 3 Average (Scale: 1 Highest to 5 Lowest)
BETA 1.30 (1.00 = Market)

2000-02 PROJECTIONS
	Price	Gain	Ann'l Total Return
High	85	(+430%)	50%
Low	55	(+245%)	39%

Insider Decisions
Institutional Decisions

Boston Chicken was incorporated in 1988. Current management invested in the Boston Chicken concept (then with 33 stores) in December, 1991, acquiring control of the company in the spring of 1992. The company went public in November, 1993, selling 4,120,000 shares to the public, and another 1,800,000 shares in a private placement. In August, 1994, 6,900,000 shares were sold in a secondary offering, with another 10,350,000 shares sold in December, 1995.

CAPITAL STRUCTURE as of 4/20/97
Total Debt $381.9 mill. Due in 5 Yrs None
LT Debt $381.9 mill. LT Interest $14.4 mill.
Incl. $129.8 mill. 4.5% conv. sub. debs. ('04), est. cv. into 35.75 sh. at $27.97; $173.0 mill. zero coupon conv. notes ('15), ea. cv. into 8.532 sh. LT interest earned: 9.0x; total interest coverage: 9.0x) (28% of Cap'l)

Leases, Uncapitalized Annual rentals $3.1 mill.
Pension Liability None.
Pfd Stock None
Common Stock 65,020,051 sha. (72% of Cap'l)

Warrants 150,000 to buy shares at $1.61

Options: CBOE

● VALUE LINE PUB., INC. 00-02
	1998	1997	1996	1995	1994	1993	Target Price Range 2000-02
Revenues per sh A	8.45	7.35	4.12	2.70	2.77	1.23	15.30
"Cash Flow" per sh	2.15	1.70	1.40	.78	.64	.05	3.95
Earnings per sh B	1.60	1.25	1.01	.66	.38	.07	3.15
Div'ds Decl'd per sh	Nil	Nil	Nil	Nil	Nil	Nil	Nil
Cap'l Spending per sh	1.90	1.90	1.79	2.47	4.71	1.42	1.75
Book Value per sh	18.10	16.45	14.57	12.12	7.49	2.73	28.95
Common Shs Outst'g D	66.00	66.00	64.25	59.13	34.70	34.70	72.00
Avg Ann'l P/E Ratio			33.0	36.1	NMF	NMF	22.5
Relative P/E Ratio			2.08	2.42	NMF	NMF	1.60
Avg Ann'l Div'd Yield							Nil
Revenues ($mill) A	625	485	264.5	159.5	96.2	42.5	1100
Operating Margin	43.0%	43.5%	43.2%	49.3%	37.2%	5.1%	44.5%
Depreciation ($mill)	38.0	30.0	22.9	11.4	6.1	.2	60.0
Net Profit ($mill)	105	60.0	67.0	33.8	16.2	1.7	225
Income Tax Rate	39.0%	39.0%	37.5%	21.0%	20.9%		39.0%
Net Profit Margin	16.8%	16.5%	25.3%	21.0%	16.8%	3.9%	20.5%
Working Cap'l ($mill)	500	400	58.9	307.2	32.0	2.8	200
Long-Term Debt ($mill)	1085	1085	312.5	130.0	130.0	54.9	500
Net Worth ($mill)	1260	1085	935.8	716.8	259.8		2085
% Earned Total Cap'l	7.5%	7.0%	6.2%	4.0%	4.6%	1.7%	8.5%
% Earned Net Worth	8.5%	7.5%	7.2%	4.7%	6.2%	1.7%	11.0%
% Retained to Com Eq	8.5%	7.5%	7.2%	4.7%	6.2%	1.7%	11.0%
% All Div'ds to Net Prof	Nil	Nil					Nil

FIGURE 2-2

BUSINESS: Boston Chicken, Inc. operates and franchises Boston Market restaurants, which serve fresh, home-style entrees, vegetables, & salads. As of 12/31/96, 1,087 stores were in operation. Provided $120 mil. convertible loan (conv. into equity ownership) to Progressive Bagel Concepts, operator of bagel shops under the Einstein Bros. name. Has 975 employees, 2,881 shareholders. Midwest Trust owns 8.1% of common; Scott A. Beck, 14.6%; Saad J. Nadhir, 11.5%; Putnam Inv., 7.3%; Chancellor LGT, 8.9%; T. Rowe Price, 5.8%; TCW Group, 5.2%. Dirs. & Officers (as Nadhir), 17.7% (5/97 proxy). Co-Chairman & Pres., Saad J. Nadhir. Co-Chairman & C.E.O.: Scott A. Beck. Inc.: DE. Addr.: 14103 Denver West Pkwy., Golden, CO 80401. Tel.: 800-480-5010.

Boston Chicken shares have tumbled as disappointing sales trends became increasingly apparent. The company assumed that the numerous coupons issued to promote its sandwich lines would be used at lunch. But in fact, customers have been using them at dinner, cutting into sales of BOST's core platter meals. BOST will reorient its coupon policies to address this. But we're mainly concerned with **the issue of product quality.** We've seen anecdotal evidence of uneven food quality, and the company press release did hint at this through a statement to the effect that "the customer experience . . . is not where we would like it to be." The service aspect of customer experience is being addressed by a new system designed to get customers through lines more quickly. But unless the food is good, customers who can't use sandwich coupons for dinner may skip BOST and go to *KFC, Wendy's,* etc. And unless food quality is top notch, BOST's home meal replacement effort (such as a joint venture with Harry's Farmers Market, which could place just-in-time, as opposed to frozen, BOST meals in new outlets) won't likely succeed.

There's been an organizational shakeup. The top corporate managers are now running the restaurant operation itself, and functions are being consolidated to avoid overlap between the corporation and the area developers. The pace of growth will also be slowed. This obviously cuts costs. (But our second quarter estimate includes a $0.04-a-share charge related to severance.) But ultimately, **we think the most important issue is whether or not it facilitates better food quality.** This will happen if grass roots area developers, once freed from such "big picture" functions as real estate development, creating marketing plans, managing payroll, etc. devote their energies to making sure that the food is fresh, that the portions are of proper size, that the stores don't run low on food too far ahead of closing time, etc.

If all goes well, the stock could be a great 3- to 5-year buy at present. But BOST's practice of being the main lender to its area developers puts it directly in the financial line of fire, and increases the urgency of an expeditious turnaround.

Marc H. Gerstein *June 20, 1997*

CURRENT POSITION	1995	1996	4/29/97
Cash Assets	310.4	100.8	2.4
Receivables	13.5	22.5	18.4
Other C	19.9	22.6	28.3
Current Assets	343.8	145.5	47.1
Other B			
Accts Payable	12.0	40.4	13.8
Debt Due			
Other	18.0	47.5	36.8
Current Liab.	30.3	87.6	50.6

ANNUAL RATES of change (per sh)	Past 10 Yrs.	Past 5 Yrs.	Est'd '94-'96 to '00-'02
Revenues	--	--	30.0%
"Cash Flow"	--	--	27.0%
Earnings	--	--	29.0%
Dividends	--	--	Nil
Book Value	--	--	17.0%

Cal- endar	QUARTERLY REVENUES ($ mil.) A				Full Year
	Mar.Per	Jun.Per	Sep.Per	Dec.Per	
1994	23.4	20.4	25.2	27.2	96.2
1995	40.1	34.8	38.7	45.9	159.5
1996	47.3	64.6	74.3	78.3	264.5
1997	116.8	120	120	128.2	485
1998	150	155	160	160	625

Cal- endar	EARNINGS PER SHARE A B				Full Year
	Mar.Per	Jun.Per	Sep.Per	Dec.Per	
1994	.07	.09	.11	.11	.38
1995	.15	.15	.17	.19	.66
1996	.24	.24	.26	.27	1.01
1997	.32	.29	.32	.32	1.25
1998	.35	.40	.40	.45	1.60

Cal- endar	QUARTERLY DIVIDENDS PAID				Full Year
	Mar.31	Jun.30	Sep.30	Dec.31	
1993					
1994		NO CASH DIVIDENDS			
1995		BEING PAID			
1996					
1997					

(A) Fiscal year ends on the last Sunday in December.
(B) Fully diluted earnings. Next earnings report due late July.
(C) Company includes inventories (FIFO) in "other".
(D) In millions, adjusted for stock split.

Company's Financial Strength	B+
Stock's Price Stability	20
Price Growth Persistence	NMF
Earnings Predictability	NMF

To subscribe call 1-800-833-0046.

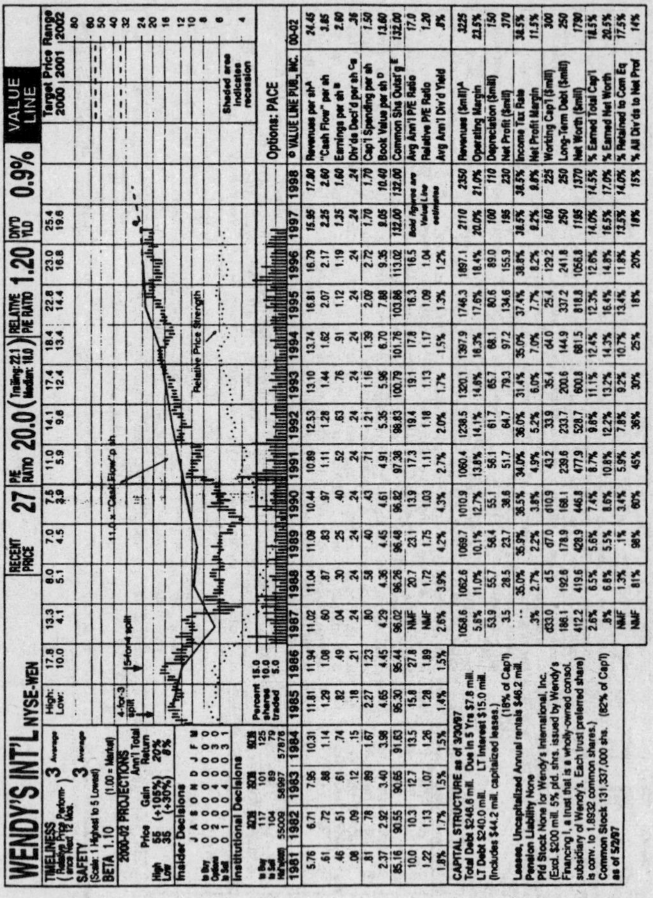

WENDY'S INT'L NYSE-WEN

| RECENT PRICE | 27 | P/E RATIO | 20.0 | (Trailing: 21.1 Median: 18.0) | RELATIVE P/E RATIO | 1.20 | DIV'D YLD | 0.9% |

VALUE LINE

TIMELINESS 3 Average
SAFETY 3 Average
BETA 1.10 (1.00 = Market)

Options: PACE

© VALUE LINE PUB., INC.

FIGURE 2-3

CURRENT POSITION (Smill.)	1995	1996	3/30/97
Cash Assets	213.6	223.8	191.7
Receivables		45.5	56.8
Inventory (FIFO)	27.3	33.2	36.3
Other	30.7	26.8	25.7
Current Assets	337.1	337.0	310.5
Accts Payable	108.2	108.6	74.9
Debt Due	32.7	9.7	6.6
Other	95.9	92.5	92.6
Current Liab.	295.9	207.8	174.2

ANNUAL RATES of change (per sh)	Past 10 Yrs.	Past 5 Yrs.	Est'd '94-'96 to '00-'02
Revenues	3.5%	8.0%	7.5%
"Cash Flow"	5.5%	15.0%	12.0%
Earnings	4.5%	22.5%	16.0%
Dividends	3.0%		6.0%
Book Value	6.0%	11.5%	9.5%

Cal-endar	QUARTERLY REVENUES ($ mill.) A				Full Year
	Mar.Per	Jun.Per	Sep.Per	Dec.Per	
1994	319.8	367.2	359.4	351.5	1397.9
1995	380.0	437.4	451.5	459.4	1746.9*
1996	409.9	491.9	506.5	488.8	1897.1
1997	458.9	545	560	546.1	2110
1998	510	600	625	615	2350

Cal-endar	EARNINGS PER SHARE A B				Full Year
	Mar.Per	Jun.Per	Sep.Per	Dec.Per	
1994	.12	.31	.28	.20	.91
1995	.15	.37	.33	.27	1.12
1996	.16	.38	.35	.30	1.19
1997	.19	.47	.40	.35	1.35
1998	.23	.47	.47	.43	1.60

Cal-endar	QUARTERLY DIVIDENDS PAID C ■				Full Year
	Mar.31	Jun.30	Sep.30	Dec.31	
1993	.06	.06	.06	.06	.24
1994	.06	.06	.06	.06	.24
1995	.06	.06	.06	.06	.24
1996	.06	.06	.06	.06	.24
1997	.06	.06	.06	.06	

(A) Fiscal year ends Sunday nearest to December 31st. (B) Based on fully-diluted shares. Next earnings report due early August. Non-recurring gains/(losses) share: '86, (54¢); '87, 1¢; '89, 7¢; '90, 1¢; '95, (24¢). (C) Next div'd meeting about July 3. Goes ex-dividend about Aug... Approximate div'd payment dates are about the 25th. Now 25th. ■ div'd reinvestment plan available. (D) Incl. intangibles. In '96: $51.6 mill., 46¢/sh. (E) In mill./adj. for stock splits. (F) '95 revs. restated

Wendy's continues to stand tall within the fiercely competitive fast-food sector. Industry leader McDonald's is still struggling with lackluster sales and an uncertain domestic strategy. But there's no strategic ambivalence at Wendy's. Like everyone else, it has some value offerings and promotional tie-ins. But these are not core strategies. Instead, this company has staked its future on fresh, good quality, food offerings. At times, when value rivals promote aggressively, WEN's top line has suffered. But rather than join the fray and risk eroding its ability to profitably price core offerings, WEN would prefer to suffer periodic "bumps in the road" and accept temporary market share losses. Interestingly, though, fears along these lines, which arose when McDonald's launched its $0.55 promotion, didn't materialize, as consumers continued to vote with their dollars for WEN's quality. Despite relatively high prices, WEN's comparable store sales gains have been in double digits.

The new line of stuffed pita sandwiches could make a good story even better and support nice 3- to 5-year share price appreciation. There's big potential here, since these are precisely the sort of products that could appeal to people who would never have otherwise considered walking into a fast-food establishment. Preliminary indications suggest that this line has been pushing "comps" upward ever before the recent launch of a national advertising blitz. This, coupled with the apparent smooth integration of the line into the restaurants' behind-the-counter operations, vindicates WEN's decision to spend so much time (two years) on development and testing.

Another source of potential is the Tim Horton's chain. This donut, coffee, soup and sandwich operation is already a powerhouse in Canada. WEN is rolling it out in the U.S. Some units will be dual-branded with Wendy's/Tim Horton's. Early U.S. units near the Canadian border are doing well. But it'll take time before we can sense how it will do among U.S. residents who have no contact with Canada. But like WEN, Tim Horton's is a quality-oriented outfit of the sort that U.S. residents have been favoring lately.

Marc H. Gerstein   June 20, 1997

Company's Financial Strength	A
Stock's Price Stability	60
Price Growth Persistence	80
Earnings Predictability	95

51

A++	Supreme relative financial strength
A+	Excellent financial position relative to other companies
A	High-grade relative financial strength
B++	Superior financial health on a relative basis
B+	Very good relative financial structure
B	Good overall relative financial position
C++	Satisfactory finances relative to other companies
C+	Below-average relative financial position
C	Poorest financial strength relative to other major companies

"Some things would send up some real red flags," says Carnell. "We want financial strength to be an A or B. If it were a C-rating—even if timeliness and safety were good—we wouldn't study it. We look for good companies to start with and keep selecting."

On our *Value Line* pages, you can see that Boston Chicken earned a B+ rating, Wendy's an A, and McDonald's an A+.

2. Timeliness (From 1 to 5, with 1 being best. Upper left hand corner of the page.) Timeliness shows whether the price of this stock will go up faster than the average stock *in the next six to 12 months.*

That's the key phrase. The rating tells nothing about how the stock will do over the long haul. A number 1 rating says only that this stock's price is rising much faster than the rest of the market now, and can be expected to keep it up for at least six months. If the stock is strong in other ways, "a high timeliness rating says 'now is the time to buy,'" says Stephen Sanborn, Research Director of *Value Line*.

When a stock's price is rising that fast, there's usually a reason. Often a young, aggressive company has come out with a new product. That's great, but no one can promise their success will last. Beanie Babies are now so popular our local toy store rations them out ten per customer. A Beanie Baby special at McDonald's tied up traffic around the block. The squishy, hand-sized beanbag animals may turn out to be the next teddy bear, a toy for the ages. Or they may go the way of the pet rock. Only time, and competing toy companies, will tell. If this small company sold stock, Beanie Baby shareholders would have to stay tuned each month to make sure their stock was still timely.

"The question I'm asked most often," Sanborn says, "is why *Value Line* will give a company a 1 rating for timeliness—and then not predict great earnings five years out." For good reason, he says. Timeliness just says what's happening at this time.

"What often happens with these new, fast-growing companies is they will be in vogue. For example, a technology company will develop a new personal computer. People will bid the price up. They'll have a couple of good years. What you have to watch out for is someone coming up with a better computer. You've got to keep watching timeliness. It changes frequently."

The timeliness rating was devised by *Value Line*. Because it's computer-generated, based on how fast earnings are growing, it doesn't reflect analysts' opinions.

Stocks rated number 1 for timeliness tend to be in smaller, less established growth companies. You have to be small to have a large relative growth rate—it's harder to, say, double your earnings if the company is already huge. That's why Coca-Cola, one of the highest valued (some say overvalued) stocks in the market, was just rated 2 for timeliness in February 1996.

That's also why it's rare to find a stock rated 1 for timeliness which has a high safety rating. Safe companies are generally larger and slower-growing. "If you can find a 2 for timeliness and a 2 for safety, you're lucky," Sanborn says. Of course, we'd still like a 1 for both if we can get it.

You look for a high timeliness rating if you are going to jump in and out of the market before the stock drops in price. But you also get them if you are going to watch the stock like a hawk after you buy to make sure it isn't slipping. We aren't jumpers. We're hawks.

As Betty says, "Investors who try to jump in and out usually don't do very well because they're forever getting in at the high and out at the low." We figure we can afford to buy timely stocks as long as we make sure they are solid in other respects, and then watch them carefully.

On the other hand, as our portfolio grows, we're not demanding such a high timeliness rating for every stock. "When we first started investing," Betty says, "we'd only consider stocks rated 1 or 2 for timeliness and safety. Now we're not afraid of 3s if all the stock's other fundamentals fall into place. We figure only 100 of *Value Line*'s 1,700 stocks get a 1-rating. The next 200 get a 2. That leaves 900 3s. Some of those 3-rated stocks are very close to 2s. They may well have been a 2 until another company scooted them out—even though the original company hadn't changed any."

In our *Value Line* listings, Boston Chicken, Wendy's, and McDonald's all are rated 3 for timeliness.

3. **Safety** (From 1 to 5 with 1 being best. Upper left-hand corner of page.) The safety rating helps us see how risky a stock is compared to others in the market. (The *Value Line* safety rating is computer-generated and doesn't reflect the opinion of analysts.) We feel safety is one of the most important ingredients in a good stock.

Safety is based on two things: first, how strong the company is—whether it makes a solid profit without going into debt—and second, how stable the stock price is. You might think we don't want the price to be stable—we want it to shoot through the roof lickety-split. But, as we saw in the timeliness section, what goes up fast can come down even faster. A high safety rating means the price is expected to rise slowly over time. Not exciting. Just profitable.

Timeliness predicts whether a stock's price will rise soon, Sanborn says. "Safety is more a measure of quality." As Margaret says, a safe company is one that's "reliable, well-managed, growing, and doesn't have a lot of debt. It has all its ducks in a row, it's stable—like a nail in a sure place."

Safety has been defined as "the volatility of a stock's price around its own long-term trend." Here's what that means in English. If two stocks cost $10 five years ago and $30 today both have the same long-term trend—they're moving up an average of $4/year.

Let's say the first stock's price climbed steadily upwards at that rate for five years. The second was more volatile, leaping from $10 to $40 the first year, falling back to $6 the next and up to $37 the next, pirouetting through the market and finally jumping up to $30 where it happened to land today. The slow, steady climber, whose rise paralleled its long-term trend, would get a 1 rating. The acrobat would rate a 5.

The highest safety ratings tend to go to blue chip stocks. Because stocks from these larger corporations are already expensive, they're less likely to leap in relative value. (It takes a much bigger change for a $150 stock to double in value than for a $10 stock to double.)

As we said earlier, we prefer stocks that have a safety rating of 1 (highest) or 2 (above average), but we will consider 3s if the stock's fundamentals are good. Boston Chicken and Wendy's both have a 3 rating. McDonald's has a 1.

4. Company debt (The first listing in the box labeled Capital Structure, left side of page.) We think the lower the debt, the safer the investment.

"It's important to look at debt," says Carnell. "It plays a big part in the safety of a stock."

You need to understand how companies raise money before you can undersand the debt rating. For example, aside from selling pies, there are two ways Mama can get money to finance Mama's Marvelous Pies: take out loans and sell shares of stock. Taken together, these two major sources of wealth, or capital, make up Mama's capitalization. We like the loans (called debt) to account for no more than a third of a company's total capitalization. To put it another way, in a healthy business, stocks will usually account for at least two-thirds of the money that doesn't come from sales.

Once again, *Value Line* has done the math for us. In the capital structure box, just below and to the right of the debt, they show how big the debt is compared to the total capitalization. In our sample,

Wendy's total debt in June 1997 was $246.6 million, which was 18 percent of their capitalization. That means that when this *Value Line* page came out, Wendy's debt fell well within our acceptable range. At that time, McDonald's debt was 36 percent of capitalization—just over the line—while Boston Chicken's was 28 percent.

5. Sales and earnings (In the large statistics box running across the center of the page. Sales may be called revenues. The top half of the box shows the numbers on a per-share basis. The bottom shows the total figures.)

Sales are simply the total dollar amount Mama was paid for all the pies she sold in a given year. Earnings are the profits she had left after paying all her expenses. As Buffy says, "Sales and earnings are most important, because profitability is the key. Without profits, there is no company."

Value Line lists the sales and earnings for the last 15 years and estimated sales and earnings for the next three to five.

We look for companies whose sales and earnings have been growing steadily for the last five years. We also want a business whose sales and earnings are expected to grow by double digits in the next few years. A small company's sales should grow at least 12–15 percent; a medium-size company 10–12 percent, and a large, established company should grow 7–10 percent or more.

To figure this out, subtract this year's earnings

from those predicted for five years from now. Take the result, and divide it by this year's earnings. That number is the earnings growth, expressed as a percentage. For example, if Mama earned $3 million in 1997, and $4 million in 2002, the difference—her growth in sales—would be $1 million. One million divided by $3 million would be 1/3, or 33 percent.

We also use our common sense to predict whether our company will keep growing. Is its industry expanding? Is the company well managed, innovative, and selling a good product? If the answers are encouraging, we keep studying the stock.

According to *Value Line*, the annual sales (or revenues) of our newest company, Boston Chicken, grew steadily from $42 million in 1993 to an estimated $485 million in 1997. *Value Line* expects them to reach $1.1 billion between 2000 and 2002.

Wendy's rate of sales growth seemed to slow between 1993 ($1,320 million) and 1994 ($1,371 million), but picked up after that, reaching an expected $2,110 million in 1997. *Value Line* says they should reach $3,225 million in annual sales between 2000 and 2002.

McDonald's sales grew steadily at about $1,000 million a year from $7,406 million in 1993 to an estimated $11,600 million in 1997. They're expected to earn $17,100 million annually sometime between 2000 and 2002.

6. Price/earnings ratio (P/E) (Top of the page, in the middle.) The price/earnings ratio is the ratio between the price of the stock and how much money the company earns *per share* in a given year. We look at this figure to see whether the company's profits justify the price they're asking for stock. It's a handy way to see whether or not the stock is a bargain.

The P/E ratio isn't hard to figure out. If Mama's Marvelous Pies has 1 million shares of stock outstanding, and the company earned $3 million last year, the company earned $3 per share. If the price of each share of stock is $60, the price/earnings ratio is 60/3, or 20.

The price of a share will always be more than the company earns per share. But the stock market can become like an auction, where overexcited bidders push the price of an item far higher than it deserves to be. Many do it deliberately, assuming that, even though they paid too much for "High End Industries," someone else is bound to come along and pay them even more. At that point, as Carol says, "the price of the stock is based on popularity, not earnings."

A stock price based on popularity and hoped-for price inflation is a little like a cartoon character running off the edge of a cliff; it may hang in the air for a while, but eventually, with no floor of earnings to support it, it will plummet to earth.

When a stock's price is bid up higher than the

company's income really warrants, the soaring price/earnings ratio should set off alarm bells.

"The P/E ratio is a major benchmark," says Betty. "We don't want the current P/E to be more than that stock's average P/E for the last five years. If it is, we feel the stock is probably overpriced." (The last 15 years' P/E ratios are listed in the statistics box in the middle of the *Value Line* page.)

"I like Coca-Cola," Buffy says, "but their price/earnings ratio has gone up to 40-something. When the P/E is that high, it's overpriced from popularity." When a company is solid, but overpriced," Ruth says, "we may watch it and then catch it in a dip, when it's in a more favorable range," at which point we snap up as many shares as we can afford.

"If you get a company that has a lot of growth, like the drug companies or Pepsico and Coca-Cola, their price will be high compared to earnings," says Ann Corley. "On the other hand, a utility that has slow stable growth will have a lower P/E. So when you look at the P/E, you also look at the industry and what the P/E is running in that particular industry. You compare stocks within the same industry. If the average P/E in your industry is 12, and the stock you're eyeballing is 15, maybe the price is too high."

As usual, *Value Line* has calculated the price/earnings ratio for us, giving us the figure at the top of the page. In this early screening, we'll use their number. When we make our final selection, we'll do some added calculations. Among our sample stocks, McDonald's price/earnings ratio was 20.4, Wendy's was 20.0, and the P/E for Boston Chicken was 12.8.

Some analysts also look at the price/earnings ratio of all the stocks in the market averaged together to see if the market as a whole is inflated. At this point in time, it is. When this is the case, it's better to buy stable stocks that don't fluctuate with the market.

7. Beta (Upper left-hand corner of page. A beta of 1 means the stock price will probably move with the market.) Safety measures how much a stock's price jumps around compared to its own long-range trend. Beta shows how much the stock moves compared to the market as a whole (i.e. compared to the average of all the stocks on any given day). Beta also is a good clue to whether the stock overreacts to rises and falls in the market. A beta of 1 means the stock moves up and down at the same rate as the market as a whole. A beta of 2 means that when the market drops or rises 10 percent, the stock price is likely to move twice as much, or 20 percent.

Of course stocks that are suddenly growing fast have a high beta. They're moving much faster than the average stock. As long as all the movement's up, that's great. Timely stocks, as a rule, have higher betas. Stocks with a high safety rating generally have lower betas.

Traditionally, we've chosen stocks with a beta between .90 and 1.10, because they're not much more volatile than the market. But, as you may have guessed, there's a contradiction here. We want stock prices to climb faster than the market. How can they do that without moving faster than the market? They can't, really. So how high a beta will we tolerate? How much volatility in our stock?

Like most careful investors, we have mixed feelings.

"Here's where we get down to each individual's risk/reward comfort level," says Carnell. "As a club, we're pretty conservative. I think most of us look for that beta to be a 1, so the stock moves about with the market. It's not more volatile or less volatile. I'm in that category. But if somebody is more comfortable with risk, hoping to get more reward, beta wouldn't matter as much to them."

That's true for Doris. "To me, the beta says that the stock can move up faster than the market, but it can move down faster too," she says. "Well, if it's a risky stock and you think it might move down, kick it out on the first filter! Don't even buy it." But, she says, an otherwise solid stock with a relatively high beta is worth considering.

"We're conservative and we don't want sudden surprises," says Elsie. "We like our betas to be near a 1. Yet we know many of the smaller growth stocks and the more volatile stocks have a much higher beta. This means that they move faster than the market; they can fall faster too. We usually consider stocks with betas between .80 and 1.20, but we have begun to buy stocks with higher betas to diversify.

"We've done very well with the stocks we have. Maybe we'd have had even more growth if we risked higher betas, but we know a lot of those new companies cannot only grow fast, they can also fall very fast. That's what we're trying to stay away from. That's also why we avoid initial public offerings (brand new stocks) and real speculative companies."

Margaret says a high beta is okay, if you're prepared for it. "If you're going to buy a stock that has a high beta, just be content that it's going to bounce up and bounce down. Growth companies usually have a higher beta. So you do know when you buy what you're buying. You know it's going to bounce a little bit in *The Wall Street Journal*. Do a little extra homework to make sure it's a solid company, and then don't worry about it. We were very conservative when we wrote the first book. Now we do own some stocks with higher beta. We wanted to diversify and get something in the semiconductor line. We own Intel now, and it bounces, but it still has done very well. Over all, it's still going up."

An example of a low beta company, says Hazel, would be the electric or water company. "They'll always be under 1 because they are real steady companies with just so much money coming in and so much going out every month. They aren't volatile."

Looking through *Value Line* pages, we find that Boston Chicken has a beta of 1.30, Wendy's has a 1.10, and McDonald's a .95.

8. Management (See 400-word analysis, bottom half of page.) Even with all the right numbers, a company can be a bad investment if the wrong managers take the helm. Try to invest in companies run by leaders with solid track records. The managers should be planning for the future and have any outstanding problems under control.

For example, in 1992, we bought Wolverine Worldwide because it seemed to us that women were wearing more sensible shoes to work. A short time later, the company was sued over delivery of an inferior grade of pigskin to another company, and the stock dropped to half its original value. We were worried, so Betty spoke to a company representative at an NAIC conference. He said they'd settled the lawsuit, hired some new management, and had completed the sale of a line of athletic shoes in Europe which hadn't done well. They expected 1993 to be a good year. Since we felt the company had handled their problems well, we not only kept our stock, we bought 150 more shares. It has since split 3 for 2 four times and we have enjoyed a 10-fold return in five and a half years.

As Sylvia says, "There are no wrong stocks in

a well-managed company. We always need to ask ourselves, 'Is this company run the way I would run a business?' "

Where can we find the answer to that question? You can learn a lot just by reading a few clearly written paragraphs on your company's *Value Line* page. No trade secrets there, but a fund of useful facts. They outline the company's successes, failures, and hopes for the future in no uncertain terms.

"Boston Chicken's shares have tumbled as disappointing sales trends became increasingly apparent," one report starts out, adding later, "there's been an organizational shakeup." It reveals management problems and potential solutions, concluding "if all goes well, the stock could be a great 3- to 5-year buy." In this and other fast food reports, they say, essentially, it's all about the food, urging investors to focus on how the product tastes.

You'll also find useful information in *The Wall Street Journal* and other business publications like *Barron's, Forbes, BusinessWeek,* and *Money* magazine. If you join the NAIC, every month you'll receive a clear, fun to read magazine called *Better Investing.* (To join the NAIC, call (810) 583-6242, or write 711 West Thirteen-Mile Road, Madison Heights, Michigan 48071.) Listed in back of the magazine is a schedule of investment workshops around the country.

If you ask your broker, he can send you analysts'

reports on many companies. You can also call the company and ask them to send written materials and a copy of their annual report.

"They're happy to send you any number of annual reports," says Maxine, "or they'll talk to you on the phone. I don't think anyone has ever had a company that wasn't happy to talk about their product. Medtronic, RPM—oh my, they just sent us big envelopes of information almost immediately."

Finally, your own experience can tell you a lot about how well a company's managed. "Merck is one of my favorites," says Shirley. "When I worked as a medical technologist, I dealt with their research department. They were studying sickle cell anemia, and they'd send us patients. Every time I called them for instructions, whoever answered the phone knew exactly what I wanted. It wasn't 'We'll put you on hold,' or 'We'll let you know.' The patient was sitting there in front of me, I needed to know what to do, and they told me. I was very impressed with the company, so when their stock was in the buy range, I bought it. Sure enough, it's been fantastic."

9. Personal observation Most analysts agree: your own observation is a great source of investment wisdom. Pay attention to trends, and to your own tastes. Are you buying more home-style takeout meals or new computer products? Whenever you find yourself using a product or service or changing your routine to swing by a new store, stop and think: is this something I might want to invest in?

Shirley really takes this attitude to heart. The day after she had emergency surgery to implant a double-lead pacemaker in her heart, her doctor found her in her hospital bed, surrounded by papers. "Ah," he thought, "she's making her will." Well, not quite. She was reading up on Medtronic, the company that makes her pacemaker. After filling out the stock selection guide, she discovered it was not only a good company, it was in the buy range. She bought her children 100 shares for Christmas. By the next Christmas, they had doubled in value. Happily, she was there to celebrate.

Adds Shirley, "Medtronic recently called me back to see who my doctor is now. That tells me this company really stays on the ball. When you see that a company is going to keep on doing a good job, you want to own their stock."

Sometimes nothing *but* personal experience can tell you whether a stock is a good buy. *Value Line* analyst Marc Gerstein says some fast food chains are suffering less from marketing blunders than so-so food. He urges investors considering fast food stocks to eat at the restaurants regularly and "place more reliance on taste buds than calculators."

Hazel went a step further. Before recommending McDonald's to the club, she dropped by the Beardstown branch for a chat with the manager.

"I like to have direct knowledge," she says. "The manager sat down at a table and talked to me for quite a while about how they hired people and the quality of the beef they used. I liked what she had to say. It was a real good sales pitch."

In the end, says Ruth, we look at the product. "We sit down and discuss it with plain common sense, and ask ourselves, 'Is this really something that I would like to buy or my family would like to use?' "

10. Price For some of us, this may be the first factor to consider when buying a stock. If you can't pay more than $20 a share, there's no point in browsing on the Intel page.

When our club first started, we didn't have much to spend. We tried to buy stocks that cost less than $25 per share, because that made it easier to afford 100-share lots. Of course, we made exceptions when a higher priced stock was still a good value. For instance, we bought 25 shares of Quaker Oats at $72.74 because we were reading such good things about it. Later we sold stock in two other companies to buy 75 more shares.

11. Optional ingredient: Personal preferences We don't have a policy against any kind of stock, but there are some we're just as happy to avoid. We haven't invested in stocks of tobacco or liquor manufacturers, or companies that make money from gambling.

"We all go to church regularly," says Doris. "If we teach that those things aren't good for you, how can we support companies that sell them?"

Sometimes it's harder to avoid than you'd think. Companies selling these products can be buried in large conglomerates, and it takes a little doing to figure that out. "I'd have been happy to own Kraft Foods or General Mills," says Elsie, "but I don't want any part of the tobacco that Philip Morris, the parent corporation and cigarette manufacturer, sells."

"Also," says Ann Brewer, "most of the time we'll buy American. It's not a real policy, just a business stance. And we have so many wonderful stocks here to select from that I don't think we need to go international." Many of our companies have global interests.

Finally, we pay attention to how workers are treated by their employers. We think bad treatment is ultimately bad for business. That's why when our local utility, CIPSCO, locked out their workers, we decided to sell our stock. Shortly afterwards, the stock took a nose dive.

Rejecting certain stocks on principle is a personal decision, says Sylvia, but you'll give them up "if you're willing to put your pocketbook where your heart is."

Test Yourself

Now that you've seen how easy it is to get the most from *Value Line*, it's time to try it yourself. Look at the *Value Line* page for Coca-Cola (Figure 1-1 on pages 30–31). On a separate sheet of paper, write down Coke's financial strength, timeliness, safety, company debt, sales and earnings, price/earnings ratio, and beta for yourself. Then give your own rating of Coke's management based on the *Value Line* report. What do you think of the company?

Well, we've finished the first screening of our stocks. Do you think we have any worth buying? We'll find out when we fill out the stock selection guide in the next chapter.

CHAPTER THREE

The Beardstown Ladies' Guide to Stock Selection

Now we come to the part of our method that puts us ahead of the game.

All investment systems tell you what features to look for in a stock. But there are so many ingredients, it's easy to feel overwhelmed. "Check timeliness, safety, debt, price/earnings ratio!" they say. "Look at earnings-per-share, pretax profits, sales!" We're left with what Carol calls "a jumble of numbers." How can we tell which are most important? How do we know what they mean?

The stock selection guide tells us. It combines all this information and boils it down to three or four numbers that help us decide whether to buy a company's stock. The guide is a two-page form developed by the National Association of Investment Clubs (NAIC) for investors to fill out. It uses simple formulas to reveal what is likely to happen when you combine the ingredients of a particular stock. If this profit is mixed with that sales trend and popped into the market for five years—will the stock value rise? The stock selection guide lets you look at one page—one set of numbers—and find the answer.

The guide looks at two key questions: First, is the company well-managed? If so, the stock's value is likely to grow. Second, is the stock a bargain today? If so, get in there and buy.

The first question is answered in sections 1 and 2 of the guide, which we'll show you how to fill out in this chapter. When you're buying property, the saying goes, the three most important things to consider are: location, location, and location. When we're buying stock, we look at management, management, and management. A company could find a cure for cancer or the common cold, and if the managers couldn't run a business, they might flub the patent and watch another company run off with their profits. Good managers will always find a quality product to sell. Bad managers could have the next Scotch tape drop into their lap and fritter it away.

That's why NAIC designed the first two sections of the stock selection guide to show us how management is doing. They do this by analyzing past sales, earnings, and profits. The company's track record is usually a pretty good guide to what they'll do in the future. If these numbers look good, we go on to complete sections 3–5 of the guide, which tells us if the price is good today. We'll look at those sections in Chapter Four.

NAIC calls the stock selection guide "the single most important weapon in the investor's arsenal." We agree. "The most successful investors won't even think of buying a stock without doing the guide," says Betty. According to NAIC, one club saw their annual earnings jump from 1–17.7 percent after they started using it, and they're not alone.

But, as Mama always said, you don't get something for nothing. Completing the guide takes time and patience. We have to do our homework. Then again, it's worth it when you remember that instead of earning A's, we're earning money.

The bonus is, it's fun. Completing a section of the guide is like solving a little mystery. After writing down the clues, you do some simple math, or connect the dots, or draw a line, and the solution—the chance the stock will do well—appears before your eyes.

"Once you get into it and find out how much fun it is," Carol says, "you kind of get addicted and want to keep going."

At first, filling out the guide can take six or more hours. Later, you may pare that down to two or three—and if you get the computer program, you can run it off in ten minutes. But if you do get the program, we strongly recommend doing the stock selection guide manually three or four times first, so you know what the computer is doing. That way, you understand the numbers you're plugging into the computer and catch errors as they happen. Otherwise, the process will feel like some kind of magic the computer is doing for you, and you won't be in control of your own finances. Your own mistakes could be driving your portfolio without your knowing it.

"Now I do the guide on the computer," says Carol. "But I understand the workings of it and I know where to go for all the figures. I know what to watch for."

One of the benefits of joining an investment club is that you can take turns doing the guide. "In a club, you put all your minds together and it's so much easier," says Elsie. "You do the homework as a club, you talk about a stock and hear everybody's opinion, and then you can buy it on your own." (To find out how to order NAIC software, start or join an investment club, or join the NAIC as an individual and receive *Better Investing* and the stock selection guide, see Resources.)

"We like to say the stock selection guide is a guide to judgment, not a substitute for judgment," says Ann Brewer.

The more you look at the stock selection guide, the easier it seems. Margaret found that out: "Before I joined the club I knew absolutely zero about investing," she says. "I knew there was a New York. I knew there was a stock exchange. As far as how it worked, how people invested money, absolutely zero. The ladies said the first thing I needed to learn was the stock selection guide, so I went to a workshop. I sat there thinking, 'Is she talking English? How can I ever get this?' I must have absorbed 10 percent of what she was saying and that's stretching it. But in the club, I learned market language, and when I went back to the same workshop a year later, I probably understood 90 percent. And now I feel perfectly comfortable discussing P/E ratios and doing the stock selection guide."

In this case, as Margaret learned, familiarity breeds comfort. Now it's our turn to get comfortable with investing. So let's roll up our sleeves and get started.

Section 1: Charting the Growth of a Company

In Section 1, using figures from *Value Line* (see Figure 2-1: McDonald's *Value Line* on pages 46–47), we chart how fast sales and earnings per share have grown over the last ten years. We use those lines to project how fast they'll grow in the next five. Finally, we plot the last ten years' high and low prices.

We're more interested in the rate of growth than the number of dollars a company brings in. There's a reason for that. If we focused on straight income, we'd just buy shares in the largest companies. A small company usually earns less than a large one, but its stock price is usually lower too, so you can buy more shares for the same amount of money. A small company, while riskier, is usually growing faster, because, as a friend of ours says, "If you start with a nickel, it isn't hard to make a dime. But if you start with a million dollars . . ."

How does that affect investors? Let's say Mama's Marvelous Pies, being a relatively small company, is selling for only $10/share, while Papa's Perfect Pastries, a mammoth corporation, goes for $100/ share. Joe buys 100 shares of Mama's for a total of $1000. Fred buys 10 shares of Papa's for the same price.

If Mama's stock price is growing at 20 percent a year, while Papa's is growing at 5 percent a year, at the end of one year, Joe will have $1,200 ($1,000 + .20 x $1,000). Fred will have only $1,050 ($1,000 + .05 x $1,000). In one year, he's earned $150 less than Joe, and if Mama's and Papa's keep growing at the same rates, that amount will be compounded over the years.

That's why we compare rates of growth. And that's why our graph looks the way it does—it's designed to tell us the rate of growth of sales and earnings.

We have to admit, the first time we saw the sales and earnings chart in section 1 (see Figure 3-1: Sample Stock Selection Guide on pages 78–9), we were thrown for a loop—but we didn't need to be, and neither do you. There's a good reason the lines

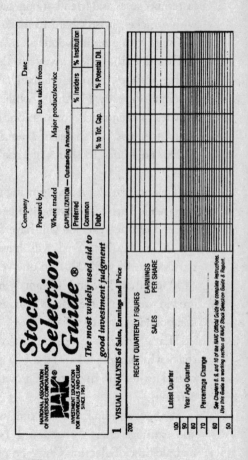

FIGURE 3-1

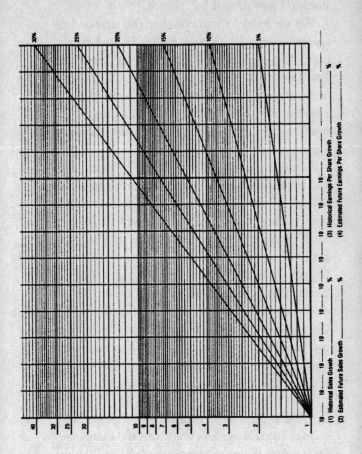

are set up that way—and the best part is, we don't need to know what it is.

All we need to know is that the strange line spacing does a lot of work for us. By making the same distance on the chart stand for larger and larger numbers as we move up the graph, the lines automatically give us the rate at which sales and earnings per share increase. We just plug in the numbers, draw the graph, and the rate of change appears.

Because rates of growth will vary between small and large companies, we think our small companies should be growing at least 12–20 percent each year, medium-sized companies should be growing 10–12 percent, and large companies at least 7–10 percent.

Recent Quarterly Figures (Figure 3-1, Section 1.) Some people are tempted to skip this box, but we do it before anything else. It's quick, easy, and if the numbers aren't good, we save ourselves a lot of time by dropping the stock right off the bat. These numbers are especially important if you're deciding whether to sell your shares in a company.

• **Sales.** Here we're comparing the most recent quarter (three-month period) with the same quarter last year. Suppose Mama's made $1 million the first quarter of last year, and a whopping $1.5 million the first quarter of this year. The company's sales grew by half a million. Since half a million is

50 percent of one million, its sales the first quarter of this year were 50 percent higher than the same quarter last year—an astounding gain.

To find out this rate of growth, we took the amount sales increased (.5 million) divided by year ago sales ($1 million). The difference in sales ÷ last year's sales = rate of growth.

"We never compare one quarter to the next," says Maxine, "because many companies behave differently at different times of the year. Their sales are naturally cyclical. Toy sales are expected to skyrocket at Christmas and drop in January; Disneyland's revenues will always be higher in August than November. That's why we always pair a quarter with its counterpart from a year ago."

Now we'll fill in the box for McDonald's (see Figure 3-2: McDonald's Stock Selection Guide on pages 82–3).

1. Find the box marked Quarterly Revenues (sales) on the left-hand side of the *Value Line* page (Figure 2-1 on page 47). In it, find the last quarter for which we have complete sales figures. On June 20, 1997, that would be the quarter ending March 31, 1997, when McDonald's sales were $2,618 million. The same quarter in 1996, sales were $2,426 million. Write both figures under sales, next to "latest quarter" and "year ago quarter."

2. We want to see how big this growth spurt was—a big deal, like Mama's 50 percent increase?

Stock
Selection
Guide ®

The most widely used aid to
good investment judgment

NATIONAL ASSOCIATION
OF INVESTORS CORPORATION

INVESTMENT EDUCATION
FOR INDIVIDUALS AND CLUBS
SINCE 1951

Company McDonald's Corp.   Date 6/20/97

Prepared by Betty

Where traded NYSE   Data taken from Value Line

Major product/service Fast Food

CAPITALIZATION — Outstanding Amounts

		% Insiders	% Institution
Preferred	3.58		
Common	689.8		
Debt	4804	% to Tot. Cap. 36%	% Potential Dil.

1 VISUAL ANALYSIS of Sales, Earnings and Price

RECENT QUARTERLY FIGURES

	SALES	EARNINGS PER SHARE
Latest Quarter	2618	.49
Year Ago Quarter	2426	.42
Percentage Change	7.9%	16.7%

See Chapters 8, 9, and 10 of the NAIC Official Guide for complete instructions.
Use this Guide as working section of NAIC Stock Selection Guide & Report.

FIGURE 3-2

82

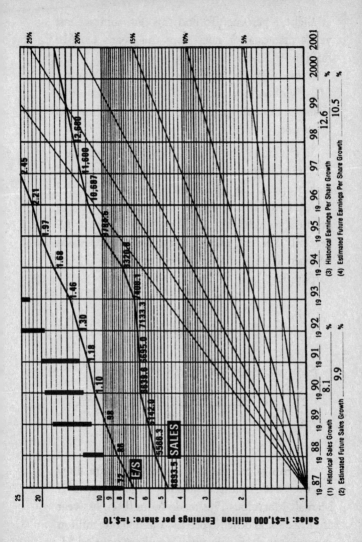

A slight 1 percent? To find this out, subtract last year's first quarter sales from this year's ($2,618 million − $2,426 million = $192 million).

(Now might be a good time to mention that for $10–$15 you can pick up a pocket calculator at Wal-Mart or Walgreen's and save yourself hours of busywork.)

3. Divide 192 by 2,426. (That pocket calculator is looking better and better, isn't it?) On your calculator, punch in 192, then the ÷ sign, followed by 2,426 and the = sign, and the answer will flash on the screen. Right: .079. That's 7.9/100ths or 7.9 percent. The first quarter's sales grew 7.9 percent between 1996 and 1997. Good enough for a huge corporation.

THE SHORT FORM

percent change in quarterly sales =

$$\frac{(\text{last quarter} - \text{year-ago quarter})}{\text{year-ago quarter}}$$

• **Earnings per share.** Earnings per share show whether a company is making a good profit. If Mama's Marvelous Pies made $3 million last year after taxes and other expenses, and had one million shares of stock, the earnings per share equaled $3.

If sales stayed the same the next year, but the total cost of flour, apples, and cinnamon suddenly shot up by $1 million, the profit would drop to $2 million. Earnings per share would fall to $2, and Mama might be in trouble.

1. Find McDonald's Earnings Per Share box on the left side of the *Value Line* page (Figure 2–1 on page 47), just under Quarterly Revenues. Write the March 31, 1997, and March 31, 1996, earnings per share in their spaces in the Recent Quarterly Figures box (see Figure 3–2 on page 82).

2. Subtract last year's first quarter Earnings Per Share from this year's to get the amount of growth. In this case, .49 − .42 = .07.

3. Divide the increase (.07) by the original earnings per share to get the percentage change. Since .07 ÷ .42 = .167, earnings per share grew 16.7 percent. The percentage change in earnings per share is 16.7 percent, while sales rose 7.9 percent. That quarter earnings per share grew even faster than sales.

THE SHORT FORM

percent change, earnings per share (EPS) =

$$\frac{\text{last quarter EPS } - \text{ year-ago quarter EPS}}{\text{year-ago quarter EPS}}$$

Sales, Earnings per Share, and Prices

On this graph, we draw lines showing how sales and earnings per share grew in the last ten years, and predicting what they'll do the next five. Filling in the graph is like watching a picture emerge from darkroom chemicals. Slowly but surely, a clear image of our company takes shape.

How to set up the graph

1. In the space at the bottom of the thicker vertical line—about $1/3$ of the page from the right side of the graph—write in the last year for which *Value Line* has a full year of numbers. (In our June 1997 McDonald's sample, that's 1996.) Then write 1995 to the left of that, and 1994 to the left of that, all the way back to 1987, which should fall under the left edge of the graph.

Now write the coming years (in this case 1997–2001) under the vertical lines to the right of 1996. (For the completed McDonald's stock selection guide, refer back to Figure 3-2 on pages 82–3.)

2. Decide what the numbers on the left side of the graph stand for. "When I teach the stock selection guide," says Betty, "I tell students they can make these numbers stand for anything they want, from pennies to billions of dollars."

For example, if we were charting Mama's sales, and they rose from $2 million to $11 million, we would make the numbers on the left edge of the graph stand for millions (see Figure 3-3: Mama's Marvelous Pies on page 88). The 1 at the bottom would be 1 million, the 2 for 2 million, the line halfway between 3 and 4 for 3.5 million, the 10 for ten million and so on up. (In each case, we make the numbers stand for the multiple of ten—from .01 to 1,000,000,000—which fits the numbers we're graphing).

If the numbers we are charting increase by a digit—as when Mama's sales rise from $2 million to $11 million—we need to make sure to start our line in the bottom half of the chart, so it has room to rise, crossing into the top half as it adds another digit.

On the other hand, if the number of digits remains the same all the way through—sales rise from $1 million to $9 million, or earnings per share from $.24 to $.92—you can start your line in whichever half of the chart you find convenient. In that case, we prefer to start the sales line in the upper half of the graph, and earnings per share in the lower (see Figure 3-4: Mama's Sales and Earnings on page 89).

For mathematical reasons, the numbers on the chart can't dip below 1. They have to be more than 1 so we can show growth as a percentage. We keep this in mind when we assign values. If Mama's sales had started at less than $1 million—say $500,000—we couldn't have made 1 stand for 1

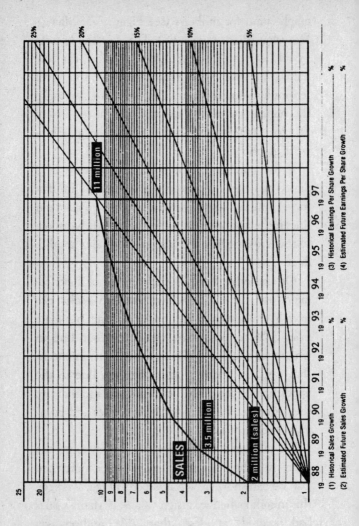

FIGURE 3-3
Mama's Marvelous Pies

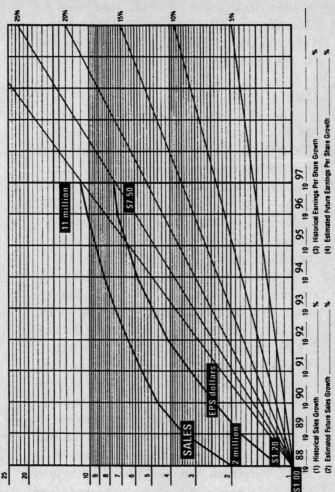

FIGURE 3-4
Mama's Sales and Earnings

million. In that case, 1 would have stood for 100,000, 2 for 200,000, and so on up the scale.

Again, trust us. This will all fall into place as we do the numbers. So let's get started.

Sales

Since McDonald's sales start at more than $4,000 million in 1987 and go up to more than $10,000 million in 1996, we make the numbers on the stock selection guide (Figure 3-2) stand for thousands of millions. The 1 at the bottom is 1,000 million. The 4 is 4,000 million. The 10 is 10,000 million and so on up. In this case, we've made the numbers along the edge tell how many "thousands of millions" we have—1, 2, or 10, on up to 100.

As you're working with McDonald's, it may help to just drop the "million" from your thinking— know it's there, but just don't think about it. You can put it back in when you need it. Thinking "4,000" rather than "4,000 million" makes it easier to work with the numbers and doesn't change the results as long as you put the million back in at the end. It also helps to write "sales: 1 = 1,000 million" in the left margin of the guide as a reminder.

Find the sales for 1987 by looking on the right side of the *Value Line* page (Figure 2-2, pages 46–7) at the line marked "revenues" (the 11th line from the top of the statistics box). Run your finger across to 1987, and you have the sales for 1987.

We find it helps to lay a ruler under the numbers

we're looking at on the *Value Line* page. Some of us even put a second ruler along the vertical line to lead our eye to the right place. If it's your own copy, we suggest highlighting the figures.

McDonald's 1987 sales were $4,893.5 million. Put a mark at that number on the 1987 line. Because the space between 4 and 5 is divided into five sections, we know the fourth line above 4 is $4,800 million. We put our dot almost halfway between that line and the $5,000 million line, and write the number beside it. Next we find 1988 sales—$5,566.3 million—and plot it on the 1988 line, a little below the third line over 5. Continue on, writing in all sales through 1996.

It may seem obvious, but it's easy to forget that on this ratio chart, as the number gets higher, the space representing it gets smaller. For example, below 4, each line represents 1 (cent or million or whatever), while above 4, every line represents 2. As a result, even though we'd put 3,200 on the second line above the 3, we'd plot 4,200 on the first line above the 4. As you enter numbers, you can avoid mistakes by keeping in mind what amount each space represents.

"Because the chart is so small, some people drive themselves crazy trying to find the exact right spot for their number," Betty says. "You get as close as possible, but you can't be a perfectionist about this."

Finally, connect the dots with a straight line between each dot. A quick look suggests our sales line is not quite parallel to the 10 percent line on the graph.

Now we draw our sales trend line. There are several ways to do this. We'll look at two.

Best judgment method: This has also been called eyeballing the data, and it's the system most people use. Basically, look at the sales line and draw the straight line roughly through it, from the left to the right side of the graph that you think best represents or parallels the sales trend (see Figure 3-5: Best judgment, on pages 94–5). Obviously, when you make this judgment, you'd pay special attention to sales in the last five years, since we're most interested in how the company's been doing lately. Where your line crosses the right side of the graph is your estimate of sales for 2001.

Midpoint method: Divide the ten-year sales history into two five-year periods. Take the sales for each of the first five years, add them together and divide by 5. Mark an **X** on the line for the third (midpoint) year—in this case 1989 (see Figure 3-6: Midpoint method, on pages 96–7). Then do the same thing for the second five-year period, putting an **X** on the line for the eighth year—in this case 1994. Draw a straight line through these two midpoints. Where it hits the right side of the graph you find your projected sales figure for 2001.

We like this method, because the numbers are more precise. NAIC advisers say the midpoint method works best when sales are increasing at a fairly regular rate, but if they've jumped up and down from year to year, the result can be way off base.

Now we find the growth rate. Because McDonald's is a very large company, we'd like to see growth of at least 7–10 percent. To find out what it is, we compare our trend line to the trend guidelines on the graph.

First, find the point where your trend line intersects the left side of the graph. Take a ruler and measure the distance from that point down to the bottom left hand corner where the guidelines start (see Figure 3-7: Finding the growth rate, on pages 98–9).

Now go to the right edge of the graph. Measure that same distance down the edge from your projected high sales number ($17,100 million for McDonald's) and mark the distance. Look to see where that point falls in relationship to the growth guidelines. That's your predicted growth rate. For McDonald's, this point falls at about 9.8 percent.

Then there's the *Value Line* method. We admit it—sometimes, instead of relying on our trend line, we'll use the *Value Line* forecast for sales 3–5 years out to determine the growth rate. "They're experts—they spend all day analyzing these figures," Betty Sinnock says. "So we trust their judgment."

Here's how we do it. After plotting *Value Line*'s projected sales figure ($17,100 million) on the

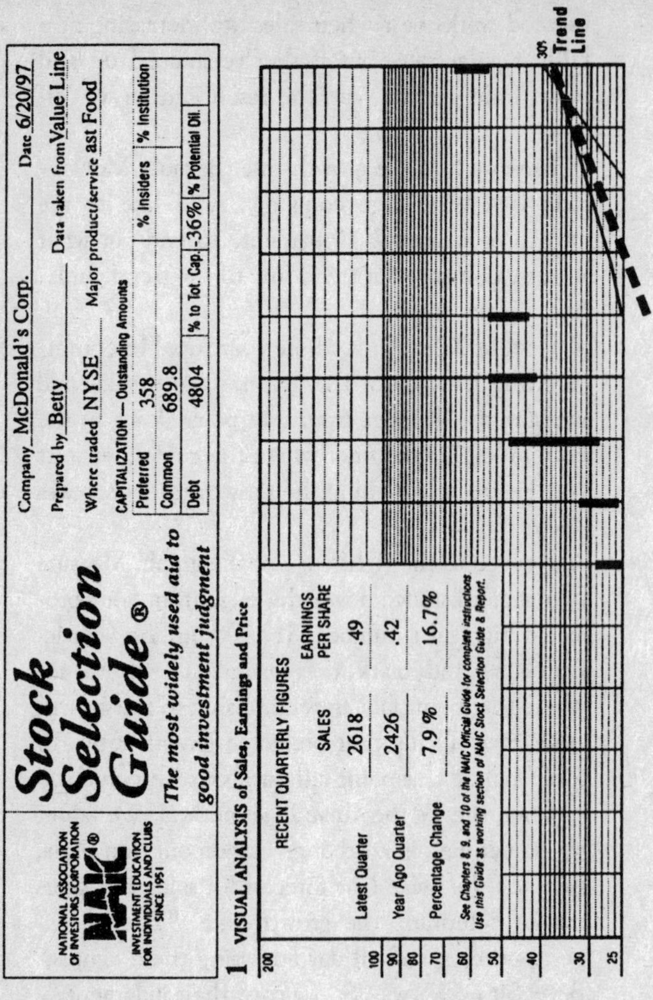

NAIC®
NATIONAL ASSOCIATION
OF INVESTORS CORPORATION

INVESTMENT EDUCATION
FOR INDIVIDUALS AND CLUBS
SINCE 1951

Stock
Selection
Guide ®

The most widely used aid to
good investment judgment

Company McDonald's Corp.   Date 6/20/97

Prepared by Betty   Data taken from Value Line

Where traded NYSE   Major product/service ast Food

CAPITALIZATION — Outstanding Amounts

		% Insiders	% Institution
Preferred	358		
Common	689.8		
Debt	4804	% to Tot. Cap. -36%	% Potential Dil.

Trend
Line
30%

1 VISUAL ANALYSIS of Sales, Earnings and Price

RECENT QUARTERLY FIGURES

	SALES	EARNINGS PER SHARE
Latest Quarter	2618	.49
Year Ago Quarter	2426	.42
Percentage Change	7.9 %	16.7%

See Chapters 8, 8, and 10 of the NAIC Official Guide for complete instructions
Use this Guide as working section of NAIC Stock Selection Guide & Report.

200

100
90
80
70
60
50

40

30
25

FIGURE 3-5

94

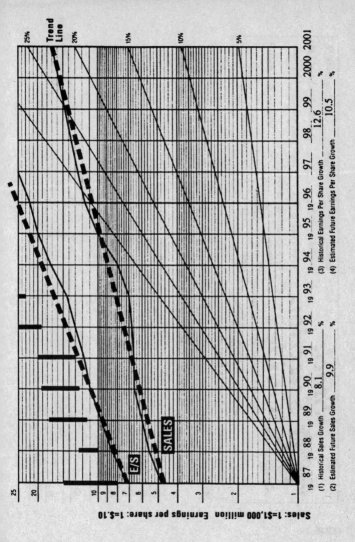

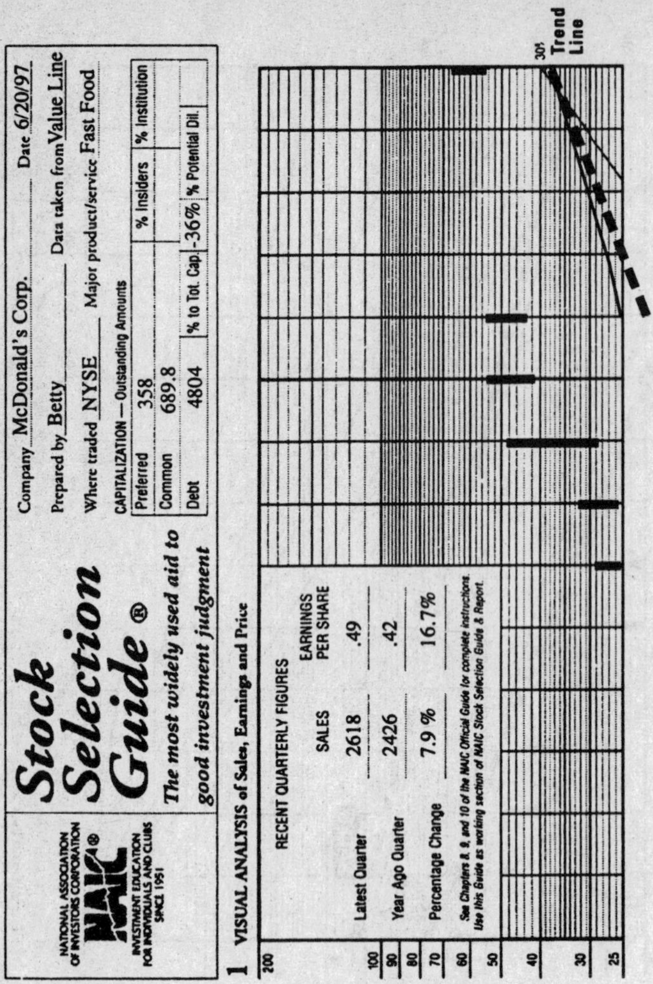

FIGURE 3-6

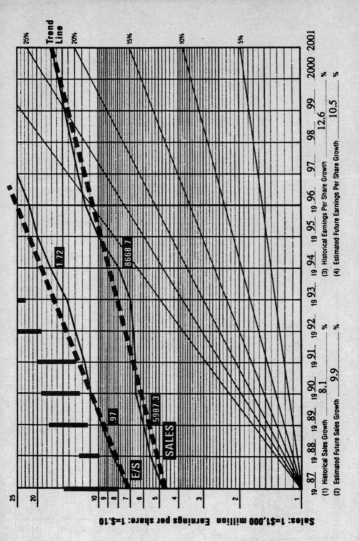

FIGURE 3-7

The Stock Selection Guide form shown contains:

NATIONAL ASSOCIATION OF INVESTORS CORPORATION
INVESTMENT EDUCATION FOR INDIVIDUALS AND CLUBS
SINCE 1951

Stock Selection Guide ®

The most widely used aid to good investment judgment

Company McDonald's Corp.   Date 6/20/97

Prepared by Betty   Data taken from Value Line

Where traded NYSE   Major product/service Fast Food

CAPITALIZATION — Outstanding Amounts

		% Insiders	% Institution
Preferred	358		
Common	689.8		
Debt	4804	% to Tot. Cap. -36%	% Potential Dil.

1 VISUAL ANALYSIS of Sales, Earnings and Price

RECENT QUARTERLY FIGURES

	SALES	EARNINGS PER SHARE
Latest Quarter	2618	.49
Year Ago Quarter	2426	.42
Percentage Change	7.9%	16.7%

See Chapters 8, 9, and 10 of the NAIC Official Guide for complete instructions.
Use this Guide as working section of NAIC Stock Selection Guide & Report.

30% 3.75

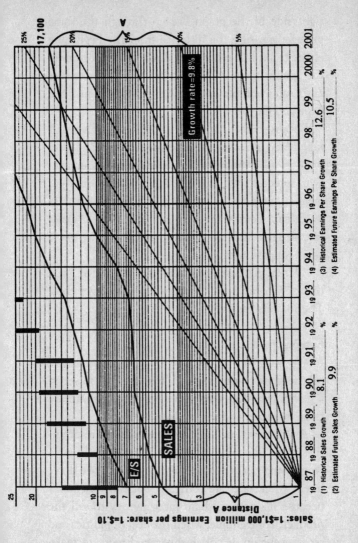

right side of the graph, we go through the same process: measure the distance from the beginning of the trend line on the left down to the bottom of the graph; measure that same distance from the 2001 sales number down the right edge to find the expected growth rate.

Because *Value Line* is predicting sales that will take place in as few as three years, their "3–5 year prediction" is relatively low compared to our five-year forecast. We think that's a good thing—it means that if we err, we'll err on the safe side. As we've said before, predicting the absolutely exact rate of growth is not crucial, as long as we get a good ballpark figure.

"When you first start doing it," says Carol, "you think, 'Oh my gosh, I'm never going to get this.' Then it gets easier."

Earnings per share

We want to plot the line for earnings per share on the same graph as sales. That way we can see at a glance whether sales and earnings per share are rising together the way we like them to.

As Margaret says, "These lines are very informative. We'd like sales and earnings per share lines to be growing near the same rate of growth. We don't like it when sales are going up, but earnings aren't because it's costing them more money to sell the product. For example, when the cost of plastics and resins went up, it cost Rubbermaid more to make the product than it used to, and that brought down the earnings. We saw that was going to be an ongoing problem, so we sold our Rubbermaid stock. Having the two lines on the same graph shows us that."

But how can we plot the line for 50-cent earnings on the same graph with sales of $4,000 million? Easy. When plotting earnings per share, we simply say the same numbers on the left stand for very small amounts—usually cents or dollars. Here's how that works for McDonald's.

1. Find earnings per share on line 3 of the *Value Line* statistics box. As we see, McDonald's earnings per share start at .72 and go up to 2.21. We'd plot .72 just above the 7 line and go up from there. We've made 1 = 10 cents, and 10 = $1.00.

2. Record McDonald's earnings per share for each year. Then connect these numbers with a dotted line (to distinguish them from sales), and create a trend line as you did for sales. Finally, estimate the rate of growth, as you did for sales, and record it on the bottom of the form.

High and low prices

We finish the graph by plotting the high and low price for each year on the line for that year. For 1987, plot the low price, 7.8, and the high price, 15.3. Then draw a thick vertical line or bar between them, to create a clear image of how widely McDonald's stock prices varied each year. (See Figure 3-8: High and low stock prices, on pages 104–5.) A series of long bars marching across the page would tell us that every year the price was swinging wildly from low to high prices. Those stocks would be considered very volatile. We'd be even more concerned if the bars weren't marching steadily upwards. We'd also expect prices to follow the path of earnings.

Section 2: Evaluating Management

Section 2A: Percent Pretax Profits

Of course, growing profits are a hallmark of good management. In section 2A we find out what percentage of sales comes back as profit. (See Figure 3-9.)

We want to know how much profit the company made before taxes were taken out. "A lot of companies can do different things to skew what they're paying taxes on," says Betty. "So we want to see what their actual performance has been before taxes."

This distortion of the numbers isn't necessarily intentional. When Cooper Tire started losing money, they automatically dropped into a lower tax bracket. As a result, even though their income was sliding, their aftertax profits looked better.

"A few of our members thought they must be

doing fine," Buffy says, "until we looked at the pretax profits. Then the numbers were unmistakable. Even though aftertax income was up, it was time to sell."

We find out pretax profit by dividing the profits before taxes by the total sales. If Mama's Marvelous Pies sold $10 million dollars worth of pies, and netted $1 million before taxes, she'd have made a 10 percent pretax profit (1 million ÷ 10 million = .10, or 10 percent).

That's easy enough. There's just one problem. *Value Line* doesn't tell us the pretax profits. We have to figure them out for ourselves.

We'll start with McDonald's 1996 numbers.

1. On line 15 of the *Value Line* statistics box, find McDonald's 1996 tax rate, 30.1 percent, and write it as a decimal, .301. Subtract that number from 1. In this case, 1.000 − .301 = .699.

2. Find McDonald's net profit for 1996 (shown on the line just above taxes in *Value Line*). It was $1,572.6 million.

3. The pretax profit = net profit ÷ (1—tax rate). In this case, that's $1,572.6 million ÷ .699. Our handy pocket calculator tells us 1,572.6 million ÷ .699 = $2,249.79 million. (One reminder: it's surprisingly easy to leave out the decimal point in .699. Don't forget to punch it in—you get some pretty strange numbers without it.)

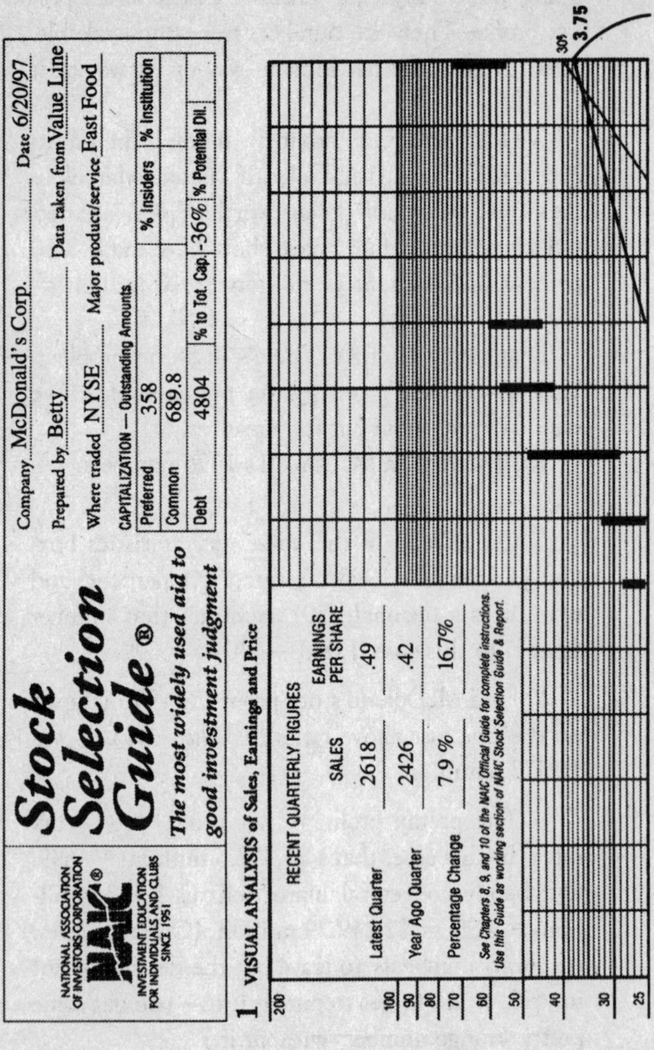

FIGURE 3-8

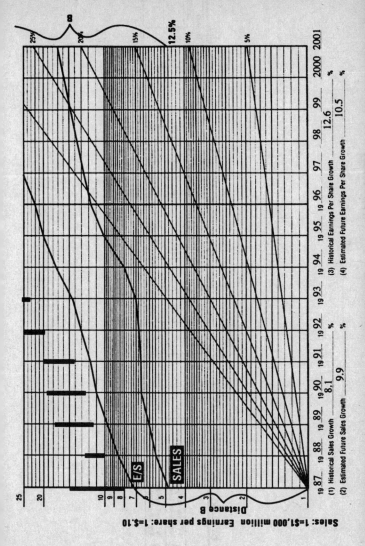

FIGURE 3-9

2 EVALUATING MANAGEMENT   Company _____

	19__	19__	19__	19__	19__	19__	19__	19__	19__	LAST 5 YEAR AVG.	TREND UP	TREND DOWN
A % Pre-tax Profit on Sales (Net Before Taxes ÷ Sales)												
B % Earned on Equity (E/S ÷ Book Value)												

4. This pretax profit ($2,249.79 million) ÷ sales ($10,687) = percentage pretax profit (21.1 percent).

THE SHORT FORM

Percent Pretax Profits

1. Subtract the correct year's tax rate (expressed as decimal) from 1.
2. Divide net profits by result of step 1.
3. Divide result of step 2 by sales.

Now just do the same thing for each year. Make sure you are using the right tax rate—they change from year to year. (One of us spent an hour or so calculating all the figures with the same tax rate before she figured this out.)

Finally, add the percentage pretax profit for each of the last five years together and divide by five to find the last five-year average. Then make an arrow in the correct box to show whether the trend is up, down, or level.

Section 2B: Percent Earned on Equity

The percent earned on equity tells us "how well the company is able to realize a return on retained earnings," says Betty. "We don't want our growth companies to pay too high a dividend, because this is the cheapest money they can use to grow the company. We like them to keep and use that money rather than go into debt to improve the company."

This one's easy. All we have to do is find the earnings per share in *Value Line* (third line down in the statistics box) and divide it by the book value per share (sixth line down), write in our results for each year. Finally, average the last five years' numbers as we did above, and check the right trend box. (For the completed Section 2 of McDonald's Stock Selection Guide, see Figure 4-3, on pages 138–9.)

SHORT FORM

$$\frac{\text{Earnings per share}}{\text{Book value per share}} = \text{Percent earned on equity}$$

WELL! Congratulations! You made it! We've finished the hardest part. It's all downhill from here. The next chapter we sit back, reap the fruits of our labors, and find out what all the numbers mean. Then we can decide whether or not to buy the stock. You've learned in one chapter what it takes many people up to two years to master. You can be proud.

And if, as you do your next stock selection guide, you find yourself clinging to these instructions like a life raft in a sea of numbers, that's fine. So do we.

CHAPTER FOUR

Stock Selection Guide: How to Know If the Price Is Right

Often, by the time a stock bursts onto the scene and catches our attention, everyone else has noticed it too and bid the price up beyond its real worth. "Shirley and I would love to buy Coca-Cola," says Buffy, "but it's overpriced from popularity. The price is just too high."

It's easy to get swept up in emotion and buy today's hot stock at any cost. In fact, NAIC says the most common mistake investors make isn't buying the wrong stock, but buying the right stock at the wrong price.

We want to buy the right stock at the right price. We want to find that sleeper—the one which is off quietly making profits while the others are making headlines—and snap it up before anyone else notices it.

We also want to buy the superstar stocks on their bad days when short-term problems make their prices dip and investors run the other way. "We did that with medical stocks," Carnell says. "We had always wanted to buy Merck because of Shirley's experience with them, but they had been out of our price range. After Clinton was elected, there was a move towards national health insurance, prices of medical stocks dropped, and we bought Merck. Eventually, the stock came back up. It worked well for us."

The NAIC stock selection guide helps us find these good buys. By taking the emotion out of stock-picking and focusing our attention on the numbers, it almost forces us to see the true value of a stock. That helps us hold back when star struck investors are buying high hoping their stock will climb higher. It also helps us see the bargain in a good stock which is getting bad press.

"The guide gives you figures instead of just feelings to base your decisions on," says Carnell. "Feelings aren't as reliable as numbers. They can come back to haunt you."

"We need to look at picking stocks as if we're buying a business," says Buffy. "Not based on emotion, but dollars and cents, the bottom line. When people buy houses—and I sell them every day—it's based on emotion. They buy houses that aren't right for them because of some little thing they like. You shouldn't do that picking a stock."

When we use the guide, she says, "Picking stocks isn't magic. It's math."

In the last chapter, we completed sections 1 and 2 of the guide, which show us whether we're looking at a well-managed growth company. Now we'll look at what many people think is the most important part of the guide. Sections 3–5 spell out "in black and white" as Maxine says, whether our great stock is selling at a favorable price.

"The main thing I use the stock selection guide for," says Betty, "is to find out whether this is a good price. I know I want the company. I just want to know if it's at a good price today."

These three sections tell us whether our stock is in the buy, hold, or sell range, and what the odds are that we'll make a profit over the next five years. (If they're not 3 to 1, we don't buy.) "The stock selection guide is the only way to find that out," says Hazel.

"If it turns up as a hold," says Carol, "we usually won't look at it. If it's in the buy range, I'll look at the price/earnings ratio and the upside downside ratio and go on a little deeper. But if it's not in the buy range, we don't waste our time."

Carol continues, "We're finding out that a lot of clubs are picking stocks because they like them or 'Oh, it's gone up all the time, let's buy it.' We don't do it that way. We do the stock selection guide. We do our homework."

"Like Johnson & Johnson," she says. "I really liked it. It was a 1 over 1 (timeliness and safety). You'd think that would really be a good stock, but when you did all the computations, it wasn't in the buy range. It was just too pricey."

When we find a solid stock that's overpriced, we'll wait and watch until its price dips into the buy range. Then we pounce.

"I had watched the Disney stock but it had never been in the buy range," Carol says. "I kind of kept it in the back of my mind, and one time when I checked it, it was in the buy range. That was an instant buy."

"But why?"

The nice thing about the stock selection guide is that it automatically filters out most of the bad companies as you go along. They just naturally fall by the wayside. But we still have to use our own judgment. "We like to say the form is a *guide* to judgment," says Ruth, "not a substitute for judgment."

We need to learn everything we can about our company so we can understand what the numbers mean and how they affect each other. Like the ingredients in a cake, they all work together and if they're not all there in the right amounts, the price won't rise.

When we look at the statistics about a company, we have to be like a persistent four-year-old, asking "why?" and then, "yes, but why?" We need to understand what caused each number.

Otherwise, we may be fooled by a number which

looks deceptively good or bad. For example, let's say Mama's Marvelous Pies stock costs $60 a share and her earnings per share are $3, so her P/E is 20—on the high side. If her earnings shoot up to $6 per share and her stock price stays at $60, the P/E drops to 10—a seemingly good sign.

But her P/E would also drop to 10 if Mama were suddenly sued for faulty crust, and her stock price plummeted to $30 while earnings stayed (briefly) at $3. Her P/E of 10 would look better, but her stock would be no bargain—*unless* we happened to know she had the problem under control and Mama's would be bouncing back soon. In this situation, the low P/E is either good or bad, depending on what we know about the company. Viewed out of context, it doesn't mean much.

Whenever a number is out of the ordinary, we need to ask why.

The stock selection guide doesn't answer all the "whys" about any stock, but the more questions you ask, the better prepared you are to make a good choice. Later in this book we'll show where to get the answers, and how to get the most from your sources, including the annual report, *Wall Street Journal*, your broker, the internet, and the company itself.

The main question your stock selection guide answers is: Are the fundamentals favorable? Should you buy this stock today? So let's get started and find out.

Section 3: Price-Earnings History

The price/earnings ratio is one of our most important numbers.

As we said in Chapter Two, it shows us whether a stock's price is justified by the company's earnings—whether the stock we've got our eye on is a bargain. The higher the P/E the less of a bargain it is (see Figure 4-1: Stock Selection Guide, on pages 116–7).

Quick review: If Mama's is making $3 million and she has 1 million shares of stock outstanding, her earnings per share are $3. If the stock costs $60/share, Mama's P/E ratio is 60/3 or 20 (P/E = price ÷ earnings per share). If Papa's shares also sell for $60/share, but he's only making $2 per share, his P/E is 30. We'd prefer stock in Mama's, because the company which is making more money per share is more likely to have the price of its stock go up.

The day we buy our shares of Mama's Marvelous Pies, we want the price to be incredibly low compared to Mama's earnings—resulting in a low P/E. Of course, the day after we buy, we hope the world will discover Mama's and beat a path to her door, bidding the price up through the roof. But the day we buy, we want the P/E as low as possible.

How low is that? One way to tell is to look at the average P/E for the last five years. Today's P/E should be at or below this average. We want our stock to be a better bargain than it's been most days over the last five years.

2 EVALUATING MANAGEMENT

Company _____

	19__	19__	19__	19__	19__	19__	19__	19__	19__	19__	LAST 5 YEAR AVG.	TREND UP	TREND DOWN
A	% Pre-tax Profit on Sales (Net Before Taxes ÷ Sales)												
B	% Earned on Equity (E/S ÷ Book Value)												

3 PRICE-EARNINGS HISTORY as an indicator of the future

This shows how stock prices have fluctuated with earnings and dividends. It is a building block for translating earnings into future stock prices.

Year	A PRESENT PRICE — PRICE HIGH	A PRESENT PRICE — PRICE LOW	C Earnings Per Share	D Price Earnings Ratio HIGH A÷C	E Price Earnings Ratio LOW B÷C	F Dividend Per Share	G % Payout F÷C X 100	H % High Yield F÷B X 100
	HIGH THIS YEAR				LOW THIS YEAR			
1								
2								
3								
4								
5								
6 TOTAL								
7 AVERAGE								
8 AVERAGE PRICE EARNINGS RATIO						9 CURRENT PRICE EARNINGS RATIO		

4 EVALUATING RISK and REWARD over the next 5 years

Assuming one recession and one business boom every 5 years, calculations are made of how high and how low the stock might sell. The upside-downside ratio is the key to evaluating risk and reward.

A HIGH PRICE — NEXT 5 YEARS

Avg. High P/E _____ X Estimated High Earnings/Share _____ = Forecast High Price $ _____

(5D7 = 3a6)   (4A3)

FIGURE 4-1

116

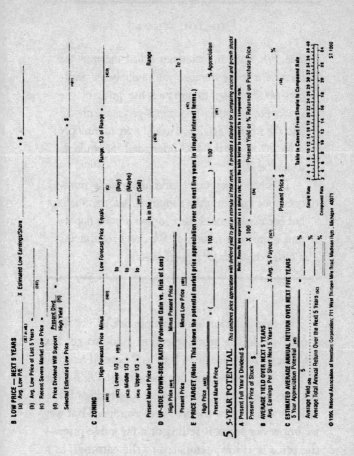

B LOW PRICE — NEXT 5 YEARS

(a) Avg. Low P/E _____ (B2 H #E) ____ × Estimated Low Earnings/Share _____ = $ _____

(b) Avg. Low Price of Last 5 Years = _____ (D7)

(c) Recent Severe Market Low Price = _____

(d) Price Dividend Will Support   Present Dvd. _____
                                    High Yield (H) _____ = $ _____

Selected Estimated Low Price _____ = $ _____

C ZONING

_____ High Forecast Price Minus ____ (#81) ____ Low Forecast Price Equals ____ (C) ____ Range. 1/3 of Range = ____ (#C2) ____ Range

(C2) Lower 1/3 = ____ (#B) ____   to _____ (Buy)

(c3) Middle 1/3 = ____   to _____ (Maybe)

(c4) Upper 1/3 = ____   to ____ (#B1) ____ (Sell)

Present Market Price of _____ is in the ____ (#C4) ____ Range

D UP-SIDE DOWN-SIDE RATIO (Potential Gain vs. Risk of Loss)

High Price (#81) ____ Minus Present Price _____
───────────────────────────────────── = _____ = ____ To 1
Present Price ____ Minus Low Price (#B1) ____

E PRICE TARGET (Note: This shows the potential market price appreciation over the next five years in simple interest terms.)

High Price (#B1) ____
────────────── = (_____) × 100 = (_____) − 100 = ____ (#2) ____ % Appreciation
Present Market Price ____

5 5-YEAR POTENTIAL   This combined price appreciation with dividend yield to get an estimate of total return. It provides a standard for comparing income and growth stocks

Note: Results are expressed as a simple rate; use the table below to convert to a compound rate.

A Present Full Year's Dividend $ _____
─────────────────────────── × 100 = ____ (5A) ____ = Present Yield or % Returned on Purchase Price
Present Price of Stock _____

B AVERAGE YIELD OVER NEXT 5 YEARS

Avg. Earnings Per Share Next 5 Years ____ × Avg. % Payout (5C) ____
─── = ____ (5B) ____ %
Present Price $ _____

C ESTIMATED AVERAGE ANNUAL RETURN OVER NEXT FIVE YEARS

5 Year Appreciation Potential (#) _____
                                  ─── = _____ %
                                   5

Average Yield (5B) _____ %

Average Total Annual Return Over the Next 5 Years (5C) _____ %

Table to Convert From Simple to Compound Rate

Simple Rate	2	4	6	8	10	12	14	16	18	20	22	24	26	28	30	32	34	36	38	40
Compound Rate	2	4	5	7	9	10	12	13	14	16	18	20	22	24

DID YOU KNOW?

The P/E ratio is sometimes called the multiple because it is the number you multiply the earnings-per-share by to produce the price of the stock. For example, if earnings-per-share are $3 and the stock is $60, you would have to multiply 3 by 20 to get the $60 price, and the multiple would be 20.

In some cases we're calculating these numbers, not because they themselves tell us much, but because we need them to find a more important number in section 4. We don't mind doing a little busywork for a good cause.

The first question some people ask us is, "Why should we do the stock selection guide to get the P/E when *Value Line* gives it to us?" Several reasons.

First, we need to find out the average P/E for the last five years. We want to make sure today's P/E is at least at or below the five-year average. That way we know our stock is selling at a favorable price—the price is as low, compared to the earnings, as it has been for at least half of the last five years.

"When you look at *Value Line*, you can look at all the P/Es for the last five years and eyeball it to see if this year's is much higher," says Doris "But when you do the stock selection guide, you're being more specific. You're adding them up and dividing and finding the real average—nailing it down. You're really being safe by doing it this way."

We also need the numbers in section 3 to predict our stock's high and low prices five years from now. Using those numbers, we can calculate whether the stock is in the buy, hold, or sell range today, or whether it's just too pricey.

"The meat of the stock selection guide is in these buy, hold, or sell rankings," says Hazel, "and to know them, you need to find the high and low prices and the P/E ratios."

In this section, the guide makes our lives a little easier by giving brief instructions at the top of some of the columns. They come in handy as you're doing the guide. We'll repeat them here for the sake of convenience.

1. Write the last five years in the first column, with the most recent year for which we have complete data (in this case, 1996) on line 5.

2. Write today's stock price, followed by the high and low for the year, across the top of the price/earnings chart. For this sample guide, they will be:

Present price: 50.0   High this year: 54.9
Low this year: 42.5

Because we get most of our numbers from *Value Line*, they are usually at least a few days or weeks old. Since we're studying long-term trends, that's fine. But when we're deciding whether to buy the stock today, we need today's price. We usually get that from today's newspaper or call our broker.

However, for this sample guide, we'll use the prices (shown above) from the day this was written. Any numbers you looked up in the paper would be too far in time from the rest of our figures to be relevant. (For the fun of it, you can still look up the present stock price and yearly high and low in today's papers to see how they've changed since we wrote this. They're on the business page, in the NYSE [New York Stock Exchange] section, under "McDnld.")

Columns A & B: High and Low Prices

1. Enter the high and low prices printed across the top of the *Value Line* page (see Figure 2-1 on pages 46–7) on the appropriate lines in columns A and B. (Of course, as you're working through this guide, you can check to make sure you're on the right track by looking at the completed McDonald's stock selection guide, Figure 4-3 on pages 138–9.)

2. Find the average low price. Add all the low prices for the last five years together, and write the

total in line 6. Divide that total by 5, and write the average low price in line 7. We'll be using it later. (We don't need the average high price.)

Column C: Earnings per share

1. Enter the earnings per share for each of the last five years across from the appropriate year. They're found on line 3 of the *Value Line* statistics table (see Figure 2-1 on pages 46–7).

Column D: High price-earnings ratio (A ÷ C)

1. Find the high P/E for each year and write it in column D. The high P/E = that year's high price divided by the year's earnings per share, or Line A ÷ Line C.

2. Find the average high P/E. Add up all the high P/Es you entered in column D and write the total on line 6. Divide that number by 5 to get the average high P/E, and write that number on line 7.

Column E: Low price-earnings ratio (B ÷ C)

1. Enter the low P/Es for each year. The low price-earnings ratio for each year = the lowest price that year divided by the earnings-per-share for that year, or line B ÷ Line C.

2. Find average low P/E. Add together the low P/Es, write the total on line 6. Divide that number by 5, and write the result on line 7.

Column F: Dividends

1. Write the dividend for each year in column F. The dividends are found on line 4 of the *Value Line* table.

Column G: Percent payout (F ÷ C) x 100

The percent payout is the fraction of the earnings per share which the company pays each stockholder as a dividend. If Mama's earned $3 for each share and paid a dividend of 60 cents a share, she'd be giving away 60/300 or .20 of her earnings as dividends.

1. Find percent payout. Divide the dividends by the earnings per share for each year (Line F ÷ Line C). Multiply the result by 100. (This turns the number from a decimal into a percentage.)

2. Now find the average percent payout. Add up the percent payout for all five years and write the total on line 6. Then divide that number by 5, and write the result on line 7.

Column H: Percent high yield (F ÷ B) x 100

The yield is that fraction of the price of a stock that is returned as a dividend. If Mama's stock costs $60 a share, and she's giving back $.60/share in dividends, the yield is .60/60 = 1/100 = .01 or 1 percent.

On line H, we're trying to find the highest yields each year.

If the amount of the dividend stays the same, but the price of the stock goes down, the relative size of the yield goes up. If Mama's stock is $60, the yield is 1 percent. But if Mama's falls to $30, the percent yield is .60 ÷ $30, or 2%. The lower the stock price compared to the dividend, the higher the yield. So each year's dividend divided by that year's lowest price gives us the highest yields.

1. Take the dividends from line F, divide it by the low price on line B and enter the results on line H.

Average P/E ratio (D + E) ÷ 2

As we said before, this is one of our three most important numbers. We won't buy a stock unless the current P/E is below this five-year average.

1. Find the average P/E for the last five years by adding together the average high and low P/Es (line 7) and dividing by 2. Write the result on line 8. McDonald's average P/E = (21.5 + 15.7) ÷ 2 = 18.6.

Current P/E ratio (Today's price ÷ earnings per share)

Find the current P/E. Sounds simple enough: divide today's price by the earnings per share. But which earnings? Last year's? If it's summertime, the last full year for which we have numbers started 18 months ago; if it's fall, even longer. The earnings numbers could be out of date. On the other hand, if we use this year, we're depending on a guess; we can't really know how many Big Macs will sell until the year's over.

We solve this problem by adding up the earnings per share from the last four quarters for which we have final numbers. In this case, because our *Value Line* page was published June 20, 1997, the last quarter for which we have all the numbers ended March 31, 1997.

1. In the earnings per share box on the lower left-hand side of the *Value Line* page (see Figure 2-1 on pages 46–7), find the earnings per share for the last four quarters for which we have all the numbers. (At this point, you might want to get that handy straight edge back out and lay it under the numbers. It's easy to get off on the wrong line.)

2. Add the four quarters together. (Don't divide by anything. We need the total earnings for a full year.)

3. Use the total (2.28) and the current price (50) to find the current P/E. So our current P/E is $50 \div 2.28 = 21.9$, somewhat higher than our five-year average.

Everyone seems to have a different solution to the dated-numbers problem. Sometimes, if it's near the end of the year, we'll go ahead and use this year's projected earnings per share. As Sylvia says, "We figure we're buying the company's future, not its past."

The Wall Street Journal solves the problem by using the last six months' earnings per share plus the projected next six months' earnings per share. And NAIC just uses the earnings per share for the last completed year.

WATCH THOSE NUMBERS

When you fill out your stock selection guide, you can use whichever analysis works for you: Value Line, Standard and Poor's, or any one you like. But whichever investment guide you use, be consistent. Don't jump from one guide to another. Use only numbers from one source to fill in the stock selection guide, because each firm uses slightly different methods to get their numbers. You muddy up your results if you mix two together.

Section 4: Evaluating Risk and Reward

Now we finally have all the numbers we need to find out whether our price is in the buy range, or zone. In section 4, we'll also find out the upside/downside ratio—the odds we'll make a bundle versus the chance we'll lose our shirts.

First we find the estimated high price and the estimated low price. "These are two very important numbers," says Buffy. "They'll be used to calculate both the zoning and the upside-downside ratio."

A. *High price in next five years*

We're trying to predict the highest price the stock is likely to reach in the next five years. We take our average high P/E for the last five years and multiply it by the highest earnings per share (eps) we expect in the next five years.

1. Write the average high P/E from section 3, line 7 column D in the first space in line A.

2. Find the projected high earnings per share for five years from now on the graph in section 1 (see Figure 3-5 on pages 94–5). It's at the point where your eps line crosses the right edge of the graph. (You can confirm that your estimate is not too far off the mark by checking it against *Value Line*'s projected high eps for three to five years from now. That's in line 3 of the *Value Line* statistics box (see Figure 2-1 on pages 46–7) in the far right column.

3. Write the estimated high earnings per share in the second space on line A.

4. Multiply the average high P/E times the high eps (21.5 x 3.75 = 80.63). Again, people's numbers will vary here, because their estimated high

earnings per share will vary. This is a case where close enough is close enough. If you've plotted your numbers and trend lines carefully in section one (or used the *Value Line* method of counting on their projections), you'll be close enough to make an informed decision about your stock.

In this case, we're guessing that McDonald's could go up to $80.63 a share in the next five years. How low could it go?

B. *Low price in next five years*

Actually, in this section, the guide gives us more than just the predicted five-year low price—including the average low for the last five years and the severe market low. We'll be using those numbers later. For now:

(a) Predicted five-year low.

1. Take the average low P/E from section 3, line 7, column E, and write it in the first space in line B (a).

2. Write the predicted low earnings per share in the second space.

How do we guess how low earnings per share will go in the next five years? Simple. We use the current earnings per share (from the last year for which we have complete figures—in this case, 1996) as the estimated low earnings per share. The theory is that in a growing company, earnings, and so earnings per share, are most likely to keep going up—they're as low this year as they'll ever be. Write the current earnings per share from line 5, column C in the second space.

3. Low P/E x low earnings per share = projected low price. In McDonald's case, 14.54 x 2.21 = 32.13. Write this in the third space on line B (a).

"Obviously," says Betty, "the projected low price should never be projected higher than the current price. It needs to be a lesser figure."

(b) Average low price of the last five years.

1. Write in this price from section 3, line 5, column B. We'll use this number later.

(c) Recent severe-market-low price.

This isn't necessarily the lowest price. To get this number, we look back at the last three years and ask ourselves whether there was a year this stock took an especially bad hit, either from a drop in the market or some bad news of its own.

In this case, we know that McDonald's had problems in 1994 so we picked 1994's low price of $25.6 (section 3, line 3, column B).

(d) Price dividend will support.

We've got to be honest here. Since we're looking for growth companies, this is not the most important number to us. We use this when we are looking at income stocks.

1. Take the present dividend.

2. Divide it by the highest yield in column H, and write the result in line B. Dividend. ÷ high yield = .29 ÷ 1.0 = .29.

(e) Selected estimated low price.

Write in the estimated low for the next five years from line B (a)—in this case, 32.13.

C. *Zoning*

This is it. Now we finally find out whether our stock is selling at a price we want to pay.

Of course we want to buy our stock at the lowest price we can get—but we don't want to be unrealistic. How can we tell what's a realistic price? How can we know when we're getting a good deal?

We've found out that McDonald's price is expected to range from a rock bottom low of $34.7 (at this point, we begin rounding off the numbers for convenience) all the way up to $80.6. Obviously we'd like to catch it at $34.7, but our chances of that are slim.

How do we decide what we *will* take? First, we somewhat arbitrarily say, "Okay, if I can get it when it's in the lowest third of all possible prices, I'm doing pretty well. That's about as good as it gets." Then we divide the amount between $34.7 and $80.6 into three zones and buy in the cheapest zone.

How do we find the three zones?

1. Find the full range of prices. Subtract the forecast low price from the forecast high price to find the spread between the lowest and highest price. The range is $80.6 - 34.7 = 45.9$. Write 45.9 in the third space in the first line of the zoning section.

2. Divide the range by 3 to find the amount in each zone ($45.9 \div 3 = 15.3$). Write the result in the last space at the end of the first line, labeled 1/3 of range.

3. To find the buy zone, add the 1/3 of range figure to the lowest price. So the bottom of the zone falls at $34.7. The top is $(34.7 + 15.3) = 50$. When a share of McDonald's costs between $34.7 and $50, it's in our buy range.

4. Write these numbers in the buy-zone spaces on the guide.

We're pleased to discover that at $50 today, McDonald's just makes the cut. We class it in the buy range.

5. Now find the hold or maybe zone. As you've probably guessed, the bottom is the highest number in the buy zone. The top is that number, 50, plus 1/3 of the total price range. So $50 + 15.3 = 65.3$. The hold or maybe zone for McDonald's is $50–$65.30. Write these numbers on the guide in the hold or maybe zone spaces.

By now, our sell zone is self-evident. It runs from the highest hold price up to the highest expected price. That's $65.30–$80.60. Write these numbers in the spaces for the sell zone.

Zoning: McDonald's Corp.

$34.70–$50.00	Buy zone
$50.00–$65.30	Hold/maybe zone
$65.30–$80.60	Sell zone

"This is a major benchmark for whether we buy the stock," says Ann Brewer. "If it's in the buy range, that's when you really get interested. If it's a hold, we ask ourselves, 'Do I really want to get into this stock?' But if it's in a buy, that's the time to go ahead."

"The zoning tells us to buy, sell, or hold," says Margaret. "If it's not in the buy range, we don't buy, even if everything else looks good."

"If we really like the company," Carnell says, "but it's not in the buy range now, we will continue to watch it. If the price goes down or something changes, then we will buy it."

D. Upside/downside ratio (*potential gain versus risk of loss*)

We love this name because people inevitably end up calling it the upside-down ratio. It basically compares the chance the price will rise against the odds it will fall.

It's pretty simple. Let's say Mama's is selling at $60 and our figures show that in the next five years it could go as high as $90, and as low as $50. We know it can go up 30 points, and down only 10. It's more likely to fall between $60 and $90 than between $50 and $60.

To measure exactly how likely, we compare the distance from today's price up to the high price. Then we compare that upside (30) to the downside—the distance down to the low price (10). That's the upside/downside ratio. For Mama's, it's 30/10 or 3 to 1.

To figure out the upside/downside ratio for McDonald's:

1. Find the upside: subtract today's price from the projected high (section 4, line A). For McDonald's, the upside is 80.63 − 50, or 30.63.

2. Then find the downside: subtract the projected low price (section 4, line B(a)) from the current price. For McDonald's, the downside is 50 − 34.7, or 15.3

3. The upside ÷ the downside = 30.6 ÷ 15.3 = 2. Write this number at the end of line D.

We want our odds to be 3 to 1. McDonald's is getting mixed results here, falling just in our buy range, but with an upside/down ratio of 2. We'll talk about how to judge these numbers later.

E. Price target: Percent appreciation. [(high price ÷ current price) x 100] − 100.

The stock pays us two ways: from dividends, and by growing in value. This section tells us how much added value we can expect from our stock. For example, if Mama's grows from $60 to $120, it's grown by $60. The added value is 100 percent of its original price.

To find *added* value, find the percentage of the original price the stock will be selling at in five years. For Mama's, it will be selling at $120, which is 200 percent of the original price. But then we have to subtract 100 percent from that number to account for the 100 percent of the original value we paid to begin with. We didn't earn that money from the stock, so we subtract 100 percent to account for it. Our stock is worth 200 percent of what it was, but we've only gained 100 percent of its value as added profits.

To find the potential earnings:

1. Divide the potential high price (80.6) by the present price (50). The result comes out as a decimal number. Write this in the first space on line E.

2. Multiply that number by 100 to express it as a percentage. Write the result in the second space on line E.

3. Subtract 100 from this number. The result is the percentage of growth your stock may enjoy. For

McDonald's 80.6 ÷ 50 = 1.6. Then (1.6 x 100) or 160% − 100% = 60%. McDonald's can look forward to an estimated 60 percent appreciation in the next five years.

Section 5: Five-year potential

This section shows us what kind of profit we'll make if all of our predictions actually come true (see Figure 4-2: Stock Selection Guide Section 5, on page 135).

A. *Present yield = (current dividend ÷ current price) x 100* (For more about yield see Figure 4-2 on page 185.)

1. Divide the current dividend by the current price. For McDonald's, that's .33 ÷ 50 = .006.

2. Multiply by 100 to express the current yield as a percentage. So .006 x 100 = .6 percent.

B. *Average yield over next five years.*

We expect a growing company to increase its dividends each year as earnings grow. To predict the average dividend per year we can hope for in the next five years:

1. Find the average predicted earnings per share.

To do this, look at your projected earnings per share line in section 1 of the stock selection guide (see Figure 3-5 on pages 94–5), and find the ex-

5 5-YEAR POTENTIAL

This combines price appreciation with dividend yield to get an estimate of total return. It provides a standard for comparing income and growth stocks.

Note: Results are expressed as a simple rate; use the table below to convert to a compound rate.

A Present Full Year's Dividend $ _____

$$\frac{\text{Present Full Year's Dividend \$ _____}}{\text{Present Price of Stock \quad \$ _____}} \times 100 = \underline{\qquad}_{(5A)} \quad \text{Present Yield or \% Returned on Purchase Price}$$

B AVERAGE YIELD OVER NEXT 5 YEARS

Avg. Earnings Per Share Next 5 Years _____ X Avg. % Payout (5B7)

$$\frac{\underline{\qquad} \times \underline{\qquad}}{\text{Present Price \$ _____}} = \underline{\qquad}_{(5B)} \quad \%$$

C ESTIMATED AVERAGE ANNUAL RETURN OVER NEXT FIVE YEARS

5 Year Appreciation Potential (4E)

$$\frac{\underline{\qquad}}{5} = \underline{\qquad} \%$$

Average Yield (5B) .... _____ %

Average Total Annual Return Over the Next 5 Years (5C) _____ %

Table to Convert From Simple to Compound Rate

Simple Rate	2	4	6	8	10	12	14	16	18	20	22	24	26	28	30	32	34	36	38	40
Compound Rate	2	4	6	8	10	12	14	16	18	20	22	24

FIGURE 4-2

pected eps for the point halfway between now and five years from now. For McDonald's, since our last full year is 1996, and we're projecting out to 2001, our midpoint is halfway between 1998 and 1999. The projected earnings per share at that point is somewhere between $2.60 and $3.00.

Or you can use the *Value Line* method. Find the number halfway between our current eps (2.21), and *Value Line*'s predicted high eps ($3.75). Do this by subtracting 2.21 from 3.75, and adding half of the result to 2.21.

SHORT FORM
average EPS, *Value Line* method

$$\text{average projected EPS} = \text{current EPS}$$
$$+ \frac{(\text{projected EPS} - \text{current EPS})}{2}$$

2. Write the average projected eps in the first space of line B.

3. Write the average percent payout (from section 3, column G, line 7) in the second space.

4. Multiply average predicted eps x average percent payout.

5. Divide the result by today's price, and you have the average yield over the next five years. In

McDonald's case, 2.98 x .14 = .417 or 42 cents. And .42 ÷ 50 = .008 or .8%. McDonald's percent payout is .8 percent.

SHORT FORM
average yield over next five years

$$\frac{\text{average projected EPS}}{\text{current price}} \times \text{average percent payout}$$

Projected average total return per year.

In section 4, part E, we found that our McDonald's stock may add 60 percent to its value (a 60 percent appreciation) in the next five years. Now we want to find out the total we can hope to earn—appreciation + dividend income—each year. To do that we:

1. Figure out the expected yearly appreciation by dividing the total, 60 percent, by 5. Yearly appreciation is 12 percent. Write that figure on the first line on the right side of section C.

2. Write the expected yearly dividend we just figured out in section B on the second line of section C.

3. Add the yearly appreciation to the yearly dividend for the total predicted yearly income and

FIGURE 4-3

2 EVALUATING MANAGEMENT

Company McDonald's

	1987	1988	1989	1990	1991	1992	1993	1994	1995	1996	LAST 5 YEAR AVG.	TREND UP	TREND DOWN
A % Pre-tax Profit on Sales (Net Before Taxes ÷ Sales)	19.6	18.8	18.8	18.8	19.4	20.3	22.6	22.7	22.1	21.1	21.8		→
B % Earned on Equity (E/S ÷ Book Value)	18.7	18.9	21.2	19.8	18.7	17.8	18.5	18.8	18.4	18.4	18.4	↕	↑

3 PRICE-EARNINGS HISTORY as an indicator of the future

This shows how stock prices have fluctuated with earnings and dividends. It is a building block for translating earnings into future stock prices.

PRESENT PRICE 50   HIGH THIS YEAR 54.9   LOW THIS YEAR 42.5

	Year	A PRICE HIGH	B PRICE LOW	C Earnings Per Share	D Price Earnings Ratio HIGH A÷C	E Price Earnings Ratio LOW B÷C	F Dividend Per Share	G % Payout F÷C X 100	H % High Yield F÷B X 100
1	1992	25.2	19.3	1.30	19.4	14.8	.20	15.4	1.0
2	1993	29.6	22.8	1.46	20.3	15.6	.21	14.4	.9
3	1994	31.5	25.6	1.68	18.8	15.2	.23	13.7	.9
4	1995	48.0	28.6	1.97	24.4	14.5	.26	13.2	.9
5	1996	54.3	41.0	2.21	24.6	18.6	.29	13.1	.7
6	TOTAL								
7	AVERAGE		27.5		21.5	15.7		14.0	
8	AVERAGE PRICE EARNINGS RATIO	18.6		9	CURRENT PRICE EARNINGS RATIO	21.9			

4 EVALUATING RISK and REWARD over the next 5 years

Assuming one recession and one business boom every 5 years, calculations are made of how high and how low the stock might sell. The upside-downside ratio is the key to evaluating risk and reward.

A HIGH PRICE — NEXT 5 YEARS
Avg. High P/E 21.5 (3D7 ÷ 8A4) X Estimated High Earnings/Share 3.75 = Forecast High Price $ 80.63 (4A3)

B LOW PRICE — NEXT 5 YEARS
(a) Avg. Low P/E 15.7 (3D7 ÷ 8A4) X Estimated Low Earnings/Share 2.21 = $ 34.70 (4B1)

(b) Avg. Low Price of Last 5 Years 27.5

(c) Recent Severe Market Low Price 25.6 (3B5)

(d) Price Dividend Will Support = Present Divd. .29 = 29
                                  High Yield (H) 1.0

Selected Estimated Low Price = $ 34.70 (4B11)

138

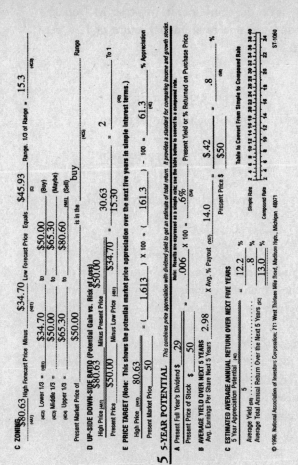

C ZONING 80.63 High Forecast Price Minus $34.70 Low Forecast Price Equals $45.93 Range. 1/3 of Range = 15.3

(4A) (4B) (4C0)

(4A2) Lower 1/3 = (4B1) $34.70 to $50.00 (Buy)

(4A2) Middle 1/3 = (4B2) $50.00 to $65.30 (Maybe)

(4A3) Upper 1/3 = (4B3) $65.30 to $80.60 (Sell)

Present Market Price of _____ is in the _____ buy _____ Range (4C5)

D UP-SIDE DOWN-SIDE RATIO (Potential Gain vs. Risk of Loss)

High Price $80.63 Minus Present Price $50.00

Present Price $50.00 Minus Low Price (4B1) $34.70 = 30.63 / 15.30 = 2 To 1 (4D)

E PRICE TARGET (Note: This shows the potential market price appreciation over the next five years in simple interest terms.)

High Price (4A1) 80.63 = (1,613) X 100 = (161.3) − 100 = 61.3 % Appreciation

Present Market Price 50 (4E)

5 5-YEAR POTENTIAL *This combines price appreciation with dividend yield to get an estimate of total return. It provides a standard for comparing income and growth stocks.*

Note: Results are expressed as a simple rate; see the table below to convert to a compound rate.

A Present Full Year's Dividend $ .29 = .006 X 100 = .6% Present Yield or % Returned on Purchase Price

Present Price of Stock $ 50 (5A)

B AVERAGE YIELD OVER NEXT 5 YEARS

Avg. Earnings Per Share Next 5 Years 2.98 X Avg. % Payout (5B7) 14.0 = $.42 = .8 % (5B)

Present Price $ $50

C ESTIMATED AVERAGE ANNUAL RETURN OVER NEXT FIVE YEARS

5 Year Appreciation Potential (48) = 12.2 %

Average Yield (5B) .8 % (5C)

5

Average Total Annual Return Over the Next 5 Years (5C) 13.0 %

Table to Convert From Simple to Compound Rate

Simple Rate 2 4 6 8 10 12 14 16 18 20 22 24 26 28 30 32 34 36 38 40

Compound Rate 2 4 6 8 10 12 14 16 18 20 22 24

write it on the third line. In this case, McDonald's has an estimated total annual return of 12.8 percent.

THE SHORT FORM
total estimated annual return

$$\frac{\text{predicted 5-year appreciation}}{5}$$

+ predicted average annual yield

What Do Our Numbers Mean?
According to NAIC, many investment clubs gather all these numbers (see Figure 4-3 on page 139), and then have no idea what to make of them. How can we tell if skyrocketing sales signals a short-term fluke or a sign of great management? When is the P/E too high? Are high earnings per share always a good thing? In the next chapter, we'll look at ways to answer those questions for our three stocks, and especially for McDonald's.

CHAPTER FIVE

How to Evaluate the Stock Selection Guide Results

Sales

The NAIC says it expects large companies to grow between 5 and 8 percent a year. We aim even higher. We only buy shares in large companies if they are growing 7–10 percent a year. With sales expected to increase at 9.8 percent a year between now and the year 2000, McDonald's passes that test.

Of course, we want to see the sales line moving steadily upward. If the way it moves is in any way out of the ordinary, we look to see what's going on. And if it drops precipitously, we drop the stock. "Each number in the stock selection guide builds on the one before," says Maxine. "If the first numbers are bad, we don't bother going on. There are plenty of other companies we can check out."

On the other hand if a sales line is climbing

faster than normal, moving vertically up the graph, we also find out what's behind the numbers. Usually, it means the company is new, experiencing that exhilarating growth spurt from nothing to something, from "a nickel to a dime," as people flock to the novelty of a new product. Because new companies grow so fast, and their stocks are relatively cheap, they provide the greatest chance to make a huge profit—but because they're untested, they're much riskier. They're the perfect model of the maxim: the higher the risk, the higher the reward.

For example, when Boston Chicken sold its first shares in 1993, its growth was exciting to watch. Between 1993 and 1994, while McDonald's sales plodded up a steady 8 or 9 percent a year, climbing up the graph at about a 20-degree angle, Boston Chicken's sales more than doubled, creating a startling vertical line.

But a new company can be the hare to an established company's tortoise. It can sprint ahead at speeds it can't sustain, and then fall by the wayside while Old Reliable plods steadily past, cranking out profits. In fact, Boston Chicken's sales line still looks okay because they have brought more restaurants under corporate ownership, so that total sales are about the same. But their sales per restaurant fell as much as 7 percent in 1997, and as a result, stock prices plummeted. In this case following stock prices would give us a heads-up to take another look at sales.

In the past 52 weeks, (including a period after the *Value Line* page we're using came out) Boston Chicken's price has ranged from a high of $41.50 to a low of $10.60, while McDonald's varied a moderate $54.90 to $42.50, and Wendy's between $27.94 and $18.25.

You wouldn't know that by just looking at the sales line, says *Value Line* analyst Marc Gerstein. That's why you have to read more about the company. "We do have subscribers who just look at the numbers and don't look at the summary in the middle of the *Value Line* page and they get killed," Gerstein says. "They look at Boston Chicken's numbers and think, 'Wow, this is fine!' But the company's whole viability is not a slam dunk right now. McDonald's has a tremendous core of strength under them. You can't say that about Boston Chicken."

If, in 1958, McDonald's had experienced the problems Boston Chicken is facing right now, he says, they might not have survived. But now McDonald's seems to be able to take any bad news the market throws their way.

The risk/reward trade-off is real. In fact, both the stock selection guide numbers and *Value Line* expert Marc Gerstein say Boston Chicken *could* end up being a great buy—if the company's new management turns recent trends around. (Wendy's, which is doing fine now, was facing the same kinds of problems ten years ago.) By staking their money on an untested stock, Boston Chicken buyers might make a bundle. "Boston Chicken still has appeal for speculators," says *Value Line*'s Marc Gerstein. "You can double your money faster. You can lose your money faster too."

We generally go with the sure thing. "I think you're better with slow steady growth," says Margaret. "You're better with the tortoise." That's why we never buy stocks when companies first issue them (initial public offerings). We want companies with at least a five-year track record.

NAIC suggests spreading your risk by investing 25 percent of your stock dollar in small companies, 50 percent in midsized companies, and 25 percent in large ones. Because smaller companies do grow faster, we expect our smallest companies, like Boston Chicken, to grow at 12–20 percent and medium-sized companies to grow 10–12 percent each year.

How to Judge Pretax Profit on Sales

We usually think the company with the highest pretax profit margin is the best managed company. It may make more profits by being more efficient, having better marketing, or developing great products and patents on those products.

A potential red flag for McDonald's was a slight drop in the growth of pretax profits in the last year—from an average of 21.8 percent to 21.1 percent.

A look at the *Value Line* summary and other sources explains why. The company had a series of marketing snafus—from the "55 seconds or free" debacle (franchises simply refused to do it) to a 55-cent burger they lost money on, to the less than stellar performance of the Arch Deluxe, advertised as a sophisticated appeal to adult taste, but perceived as simply overpriced. Meanwhile they have the Big Mac, one of the best brands in corporate history because of its name recognition. Gerstein says, "They can't make money on it. They've run so many reduced-price specials, no one is willing to pay full price anymore and they're selling it nearly at cost."

As a result, while sales have continued to increase, profits have grown slightly less quickly. But, says Gerstein, he's bullish on McDonald's.

"You always have to look at what news the market is missing," he says. In McDonald's case, people don't realize that McDonald's knows its customer base. Their customers are less concerned with gourmet food than with convenience, low prices, and a fun place to take children. Because they have the most restaurants of any fast food chain, they're more likely to be the store just around the corner when you need a quick bite. Maybe more important, he says, for all their mistakes, McDonald's seems to have a strong management. "They're very fast to recognize a mistake. They were quick to yank 'Campaign '55' (a celebration of the year they were founded). A management that acknowledges problems, I respect," he says. They've also streamlined management procedures.

McDonald's is in an uptrend, according to Gerstein, because "the company has digested so much bad news and the stock is still standing there."

Or as Ann Corley says, "Sometimes when you're that big, you can have bad news and still be ahead of the others, because you're so far ahead to begin with."

Shirley agrees. "We have a McDonald's here in town," she says. "They are a well-managed company. They have rules. It stands. They do a good job. If you go to eat at McDonald's you know exactly what caliber of food you're going to get. It's always the same all over the country. It's always a good hamburger every time you go. So you look at these companies and ask what they're doing—is it going to be a good thing? McDonald's is going to be in existence for a long time. It's a good stock."

Finally, Gerstein says, "McDonald's is big overseas. They're way ahead of the pack over there." Americans, he says, often forget to take these foreign markets into account.

And when you're selling in such volume— McDonald's sells more hamburgers than any other fast food chain—maybe you can afford slightly less profit per burger.

"We don't use pretax profit as a final criteria," says Carnell. "If a company is great in all other respects, it doesn't stop us. With McDonald's, we figure profits are so high in the first place, if they go down a little bit, it's still okay. We know in any business there are times when this happens. When the company is making $11,000 million to start with, we figure the difference between 21.1 percent growth, and 21.8 percent growth is probably not going to matter."

How much profit a company can be expected to make varies from industry to industry, so we should compare these figures within an industry. The fast food industry is very competitive. There are so many different chains springing up, each one has to scramble for dining dollars. As a result, how McDonald's profit compares to Wendy's is significant. How it stacks up against Pacific Gas and Electric is not.

We encourage you to fill out the blank stock selection guides for Wendy's and Boston Chicken for yourselves. (See Figures 5-2 through 5-7.) The blank guides can be found on pages 148–51 (see Figure 5-1), and their *Value Line* pages on pages 48 through 51.

Earnings Per Share
It's one of the harsh realities of business—you only make money as fast as you sell the product. Since

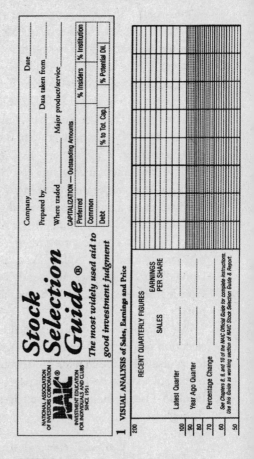

FIGURE 5-1

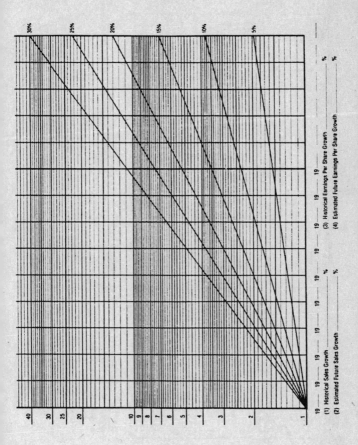

2 EVALUATING MANAGEMENT   Company

	19__	19__	19__	19__	19__	LAST 5 YEAR AVG.	TREND UP	TREND DOWN
A % Pre-tax Profit on Sales (Net Before Taxes ÷ Sales)								
B % Earned on Equity (E/S ÷ Book Value)								

3 PRICE-EARNINGS HISTORY as an indicator of the future

This shows how stock prices have fluctuated with earnings and dividends. It is a building block for translating earnings into future stock prices.

Year	PRESENT PRICE A PRICE HIGH	B LOW	HIGH THIS YEAR C Earnings Per Share	D Price Earnings Ratio HIGH A÷C	E Price Earnings Ratio LOW B÷C	LOW THIS YEAR Dividend Per Share	F % Payout F÷C X 100	G % High Yield F÷B X 100	H
1									
2									
3									
4									
5									
6 TOTAL									
7 AVERAGE									
8 AVERAGE PRICE EARNINGS RATIO				9 CURRENT PRICE EARNINGS RATIO					

4 EVALUATING RISK and REWARD over the next 5 years

Assuming one recession and one business boom every 5 years, calculations are made of how high and how low the stock might sell. The upside-downside ratio is the key to evaluating risk and reward.

A HIGH PRICE — NEXT 5 YEARS

Avg. High P/E _____ (3D7 as ad.) X Estimated High Earnings/Share _____ = Forecast High Price $ _____ (4A1)

B LOW PRICE — NEXT 5 YEARS

(a) Avg. Low P/E _____ (3E7 as ad.) X Estimated Low Earnings/Share _____ = $ _____ (3B7)

(b) Avg. Low Price of Last 5 Years _____

(c) Recent Severe Market Low Price _____

(d) Price Dividend Will Support $\dfrac{\text{Present Divd.}}{\text{High Yield (H)}}$ _____ = = $ _____

Selected Estimated Low Price _____ = $ _____ (4B1)

FIGURE 5-1, cont.

C ZONING

High Forecast Price _____ Minus _____ Low Forecast Price _____ Equals _____ (C) _____ Range. 1/3 of Range = _____ (4C6)
    (4A5)   (4B1)

   (4C2) Lower 1/3 = _____ to _____ (Buy)

   (4C3) Middle 1/3 = _____ to _____ (Maybe)

   (4C4) Upper 1/3 = _____ to _____ (4B1) (Sell)

Present Market Price of _____ is in the _____ _____ Range
                                                              (4C5)

D UP-SIDE DOWN-SIDE RATIO (Potential Gain vs. Risk of Loss)

$$\frac{\text{High Price (4A5)} \quad \text{Minus Present Price}}{\text{Present Price} \quad \text{Minus Low Price (4B1)}} = \text{_____} \quad \text{To 1}_{(4D)}$$

E PRICE TARGET (Note: This shows the potential market price appreciation over the next five years in simple interest terms.)

$$\frac{\text{High Price (4A5)}}{\text{Present Market Price}} = (\text{_____}) \times 100 = (\text{_____}) - 100 = \text{_____} \%\ \text{Appreciation}_{(4E)}$$

5 5-YEAR POTENTIAL.

This combines *price appreciation with dividend yield* to get an estimate of total return. *It provides a standard for comparing income and growth stocks.*

Note: Results are expressed as a simple rate; use the table below to convert to a compound rate.

A Present Full Year's Dividend $ _____

$$\frac{\text{Present Full Year's Dividend \$}}{\text{Present Price of Stock \$}} \times 100 = \text{_____}_{(5A)} \quad \text{Present Yield or \% Returned on Purchase Price}$$

B AVERAGE YIELD OVER NEXT 5 YEARS

$$\frac{\text{Avg. Earnings Per Share Next 5 Years} \times \text{Avg. \% Payout}_{(5B7)}}{\text{Present Price \$}} = \text{_____}_{(5B)} \quad \%$$

C ESTIMATED AVERAGE ANNUAL RETURN OVER NEXT FIVE YEARS

$$\frac{\text{5 Year Appreciation Potential}_{(4E)}}{5} = \text{_____} \%$$

Average Yield (5B) .... _____ %

Average Total Annual Return Over the Next 5 Years (5C) .... _____ %

Table to Convert From Simple to Compound Rate																	
Simple Rate	2	4	6	8	10	12	14	16	18	20	22	24	26	28	30	32	34	36	38	40
Compound Rate	2	4	6	8	9	11	12	14	16	18	20	22	24

© 1990, National Association of Investors Corporation; 711 West Thirteen Mile Road, Madison Hgts., Michigan 48071

ST-1060

151

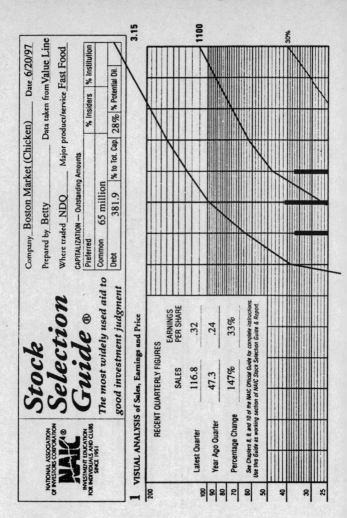

FIGURE 5-2

152

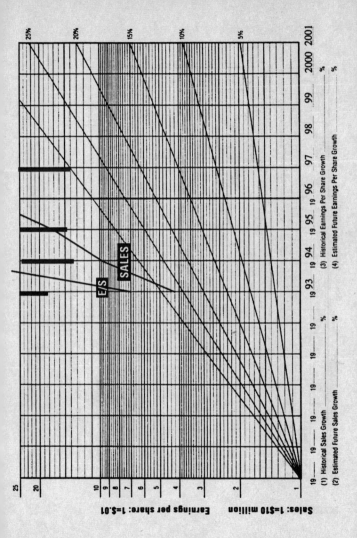

Company _____ Boston Market (Chicken)

2 EVALUATING MANAGEMENT

	19 88	19 89	19 90	19 91	19 92	19 93	19 94	19 95	19 96	19 97	LAST 5 YEAR AVG.	TREND UP	DOWN
A % Pre-tax Profit on Sales (Net Before Taxes ÷ Sales)						2.6	21.3	34.1	40.4	27	30.7		↓
B % Earned on Equity (E/S ÷ Book Value)							5.1	5.4	6.9	7.6	5.5	↑	

3 PRICE-EARNINGS HISTORY as an indicator of the future

This shows how stock prices have fluctuated with earnings and dividends. It is a building block for translating earnings into future stock prices.

Year	A PRESENT PRICE		B C Earnings Per Share	D Price Earnings Ratio		E Low B÷C	F Dividend Per Share	G % Payout F÷C X 100	H % High Yield F÷B X 100
	HIGH	LOW		HIGH A÷C	HIGH THIS YEAR 16.5	LOW THIS YEAR 14			
1 1994	24.3	13.5	.38	63.9	35.5				
2 1995	35.9	14.5	.66	54.4	22.0				
3 1996	41.5	24.1	1.01	41.1	23.9				
4 1997	38.3	14.0	1.25	30.6	11.2				
5									
6 TOTAL				47.5	23.2				
7 AVERAGE	16.5								
8 AVERAGE PRICE EARNINGS RATIO							9 CURRENT PRICE EARNINGS RATIO		

(Column headers above the E section read: "HIGH THIS YEAR 58.3" and "LOW THIS YEAR 14")

4 EVALUATING RISK and REWARD over the next 5 years

Assuming one recession and one business boom every 5 years, calculations are made of how high and how low the stock might sell. The upside-downside ratio is the key to evaluating risk and reward.

A HIGH PRICE — NEXT 5 YEARS
Avg. High P/E 47.5 X Estimated High Earnings/Share 3.15 = Forecast High Price $ 149.62 (4A1)
   (3E7 or 4A)

B LOW PRICE — NEXT 5 YEARS
Avg. Low P/E 23.2 X Estimated Low Earnings/Share 1.25 = $ 29
   (3E7 or 4B)

(a) Avg. Low P/E 16.5
(b) Avg. Low Price of Last 5 Years 16.5
(c) Recent Severe Market Low Price 14.0
(d) Price Dividend Will Support Present Dvd. = $ 29
                                  High Yield (H)   (4B1)

Selected Estimated Low Price

FIGURE 5-2, cont.

C ZONING 149.62 High Forecast Price Minus 29 Low Forecast Price Equals 120.62 Range. 1/3 of Range = 40.21

(4A1) (4B1) (4C) (4D2)

(4C2) Lower 1/3 = (4B1) 29.00 to 69.21 (Buy)

(4C3) Middle 1/3 = 69.21 to 109.42 (Maybe)

(4C4) Upper 1/3 = 109.42 to 149.62 (4E1) (Sell)

Present Market Price of 16 is in the buy Range

(4C5)

D UP-SIDE DOWN-SIDE RATIO (Potential Gain vs. Risk of Loss)

High Price (4A1) 149.62 Minus Present Price 16 = 136.6 = more than 136* To 1

Present Price 16 Minus Low Price (4B1) 29 -13 (4C)

E PRICE TARGET (Note: This shows the potential market price appreciation over the next five years in simple interest terms.)

High Price (4A1) 149.62 = (93.5) X 100 = (935) - 100 = 835 % Appreciation

Present Market Price 16 (4D) (4E)

5 5-YEAR POTENTIAL *This combines price appreciation with dividend yield to get an estimate of total return. It provides a standard for comparing income and growth stocks.*

A Present Full Year's Dividend $ ____ = ____ X 100 = ____ Present Yield or % Returned on Purchase Price

Present Price of Stock $ (5A) (5A1)

B AVERAGE YIELD OVER NEXT 5 YEARS

Avg. Earnings Per Share Next 5 Years ____ X Avg. % Payout (5A7) ____ = ____ %

Note: Results are expressed as a simple rate; use the table below to convert to a compound rate.

Present Price $ (5B)

C ESTIMATED AVERAGE ANNUAL RETURN OVER NEXT FIVE YEARS

5 Year Appreciation Potential (4E) ____ %

Average Yield (5B) 5 ____ %

Average Total Annual Return Over the Next 5 Years (5C2) ____ %

Table to Convert From Simple to Compound Rate

Simple Rate | 2 | 4 | 6 | 8 | 10 12 | 14 16 | 18 | 20 22 24 26 28 30 32 34 36 38 40

Compound Rate | 2 | 4 | 5 | 6 | 8 | 9 | 10 | 12 | 14 | 16 | 18 | 20 | 22 | 24

© 1996, National Association of Investors Corporation; 711 West Thirteen Mile Road, Madison Hgts., Michigan 48071   SI-1060

* Because the present price is lower than possible estimated future price, the numbers are skewed.

Stock Selection Guide ®

NATIONAL ASSOCIATION OF INVESTORS CORPORATION

NAIC®
INVESTMENT EDUCATION FOR INDIVIDUALS AND CLUBS SINCE 1951

The most widely used aid to good investment judgment

Company __Boston Market (Chicken)__ Date 6/20/97

Prepared by __Betty__ Data taken from __Value Line__

Where traded __NDQ__ Major product/service __Fast Food__

CAPITALIZATION — Outstanding Amounts

Preferred		% Insiders	% Institution
Common	65 million		
Debt	381.9	% to Tot. Cap 28%	% Potential Dil.

3.15

Growth rate: 30%

1100

30%

1 VISUAL ANALYSIS of Sales, Earnings and Price

RECENT QUARTERLY FIGURES

	SALES	EARNINGS PER SHARE
Latest Quarter	116.8	.32
Year Ago Quarter	47.3	.24
Percentage Change	147%	33%

See Chapters 8, 9, and 10 of the NAIC Official Guide for complete instructions. Use this Guide as working section of NAIC Stock Selection Guide & Report.

200

100
90
80
70
60
50

40

30

25

FIGURE 5-3

156

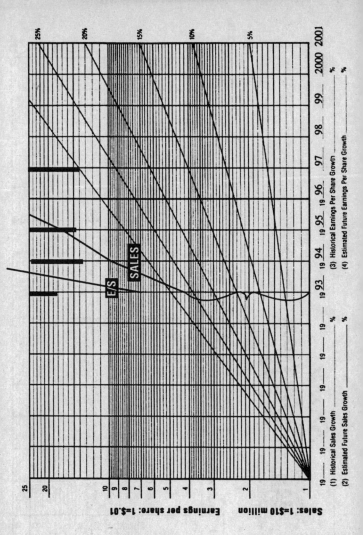

(1) Historical Sales Growth _____ %

(2) Estimated Future Sales Growth _____ %

(3) Historical Earnings Per Share Growth _____ %

(4) Estimated Future Earnings Per Share Growth _____ %

Sales: 1=$10 million   Earnings per share: 1=$.01

157

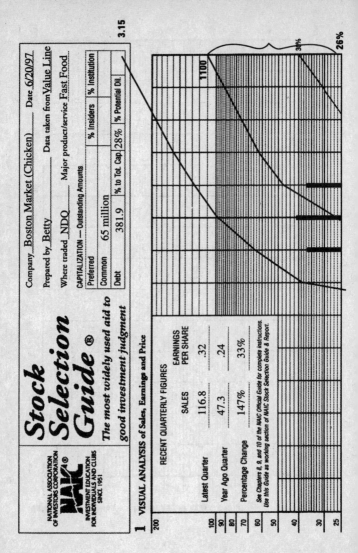

FIGURE 5-4

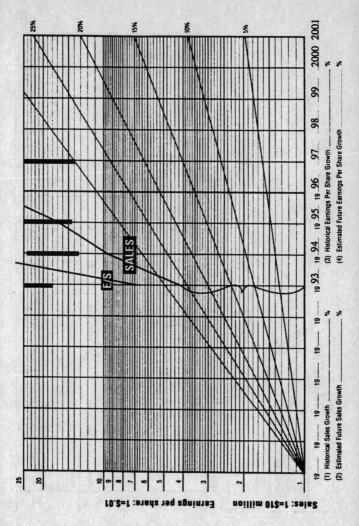

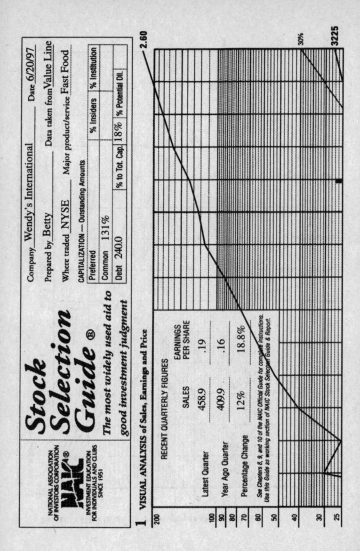

FIGURE 5-5

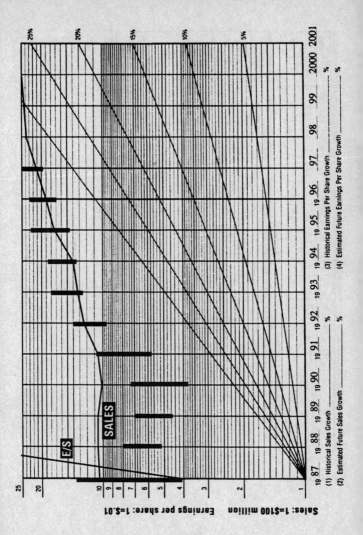

Company __Wendy's__

2 EVALUATING MANAGEMENT

	19 87	19 88	19 89	19 90	19 91	19 92	19 93	19 94	19 95	19 96	LAST 5 YEAR AVG.	TREND UP	DOWN
A % Pre-tax Profit on Sales (Net Before Taxes ÷ Sales)	—	4.1	3.5	6.0	7.4	8.2	8.8	10.7	12.3	13.4	10.7	↑	
B % Earned on Equity (E/S ÷ Book Value)	.9	6.9	5.6	8.7	10.6	11.8	12.8	13.6	14.2	12.7	13.0		→

3 PRICE-EARNINGS HISTORY as an indicator of the future

This shows how stock prices have fluctuated with earnings and dividends. It is a building block for translating earnings into future stock prices.

PRESENT PRICE 27 HIGH THIS YEAR 27 LOW THIS YEAR 19.6

	Year	A PRICE HIGH	B LOW	C Earnings Per Share	D Price Earnings Ratio HIGH A÷C	E LOW B÷C	F Dividend Per Share	G % Payout F÷C X 100	H % High Yield F÷B X 100
1	1992	14.1	9.6	.63	22.4	15.2	.24	38.1	2.5
2	1993	17.4	12.4	.76	22.9	16.3	.24	31.6	1.9
3	1994	18.4	13.4	.91	20.2	14.7	.24	26.4	1.8
4	1995	22.8	14.4	1.12	20.4	12.9	.24	21.4	1.7
5	1996	23.0	16.8	1.19	19.3	14.1	.24	20.2	1.4
6	TOTAL								
7	AVERAGE		13.3		21.0	14.6		27.5	
8	AVERAGE PRICE EARNINGS RATIO		17.8						
9					CURRENT PRICE EARNINGS RATIO		22.1		

4 EVALUATING RISK and REWARD over the next 5 years

Assuming one recession and one business boom every 5 years, calculations are made of how high and how low the stock might sell. The upside-downside ratio is the key to evaluating risk and reward.

A HIGH PRICE — NEXT 5 YEARS
Avg. High P/E __21__ (3RD yr. H4) x Estimated High Earnings/Share __2.60__ = Forecast High Price $ __54.6__ (4A1)

B LOW PRICE — NEXT 5 YEARS
(a) Avg. Low P/E __14.6__ (B7 or H4) x Estimated Low Earnings/Share __1.19__ = $ __17.4__
(b) Avg. Low Price of Last 5 Years __13.3__
(c) Recent Severe Market Low Price __13.4__
(d) Price Dividend Will Support: Present Divd. __.24__ / High Yield (H) __.096__ = __2.5__
Selected Estimated Low Price ____ = $ __17.4__ (4B1)

FIGURE 5-5, cont.

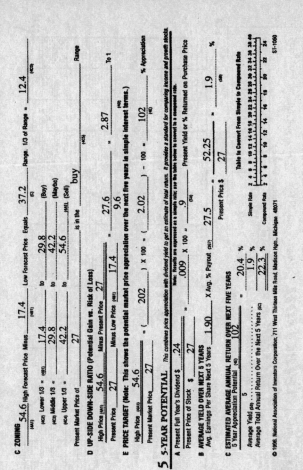

C ZONING 54.6 High Forecast Price Minus 17.4 Low Forecast Price Equals 37.2 Range. 1/3 of Range = 12.4
(4A) (4B1) (C) (4C3)

(4C2) Lower 1/3 = (4B1)   17.4   to   29.8   (Buy)
(4C2) Middle 1/3 =   29.8   to   42.2   (Maybe)
(4C4) Upper 1/3 =   42.2   to   54.6   (4B1) (Sell)

Present Market Price of   27   is in the   buy   Range
(4C3)

D UP-SIDE DOWN-SIDE RATIO (Potential Gain vs. Risk of Loss)

High Price (4B1)   54.6   Minus Present Price   27
= ────────────────────────────────── = 27.6 = 2.87 To 1
Present Price   27   Minus Low Price (4B1)   17.4   9.6 (4D)

E PRICE TARGET (Note: This shows the potential market price appreciation over the next five years in simple interest terms.)

High Price (4B3)   54.6
───────────────── = (202) X 100 = (2.02) – 100 = 102 % Appreciation
Present Market Price   27 (4E)

5 5-YEAR POTENTIAL *This combines price appreciation with dividend yield to get an estimate of total return. It provides a standard for comparing income and growth stocks.*

Note: Results are expressed as a simple rate; see the table below to convert to a compound rate.

A Present Full Year's Dividend $ .24
──────────────────────────── = .009 X 100 = .9 Present Yield or % Returned on Purchase Price
Present Price of Stock $ 27 (5A)

B AVERAGE YIELD OVER NEXT 5 YEARS
Avg. Earnings Per Share Next 5 Years   1.90   X Avg. % Payout (5B7) 27.5 = 52.25 = 1.9 %
──────────────────────
Present Price $ 27 (5B)

C ESTIMATED AVERAGE ANNUAL RETURN OVER NEXT FIVE YEARS
5 Year Appreciation Potential (4E)   102
─────────────────────────────── = 20.4 %
5

Average Yield (5B)   1.9 %
Average Total Annual Return Over the Next 5 Years (5C)   22.3 %

Table to Convert From Simple to Compound Rate

Simple Rate   2 4 6 8 10 12 14 16 18 20 22 24 26 28 30 32 34 36 38 40
Compound Rate 2 4 6 8 10 12 14 16 18 20 22 24

© 1996. National Association of Investors Corporation, 711 West Thirteen Mile Road, Madison Hgts., Michigan 48071

ST-1060

NATIONAL ASSOCIATION
OF INVESTORS CORPORATION

NAIC®

INVESTMENT EDUCATION
FOR INDIVIDUALS AND CLUBS
SINCE 1951

Stock Selection Guide ®

The most widely used aid to good investment judgment

Company **Wendy's International**   Date **6/20/97**

Prepared by **Betty**   Data taken from **Value Line**

Where traded **NYSE**   Major product/service **Fast Food**

CAPITALIZATION — Outstanding Amounts

Preferred		% Insiders	% Institution
Common **131%**			
Debt **240.0**	% to Tot. Cap) **18%**	% Potential Dil.	

1 VISUAL ANALYSIS of Sales, Earnings and Price

RECENT QUARTERLY FIGURES

	SALES	EARNINGS PER SHARE
Latest Quarter	458.9	.19
Year Ago Quarter	409.9	.16
Percentage Change	12%	18.8%

See Chapters 8, 9, and 10 of the NAIC Official Guide for complete instructions.
Use this Guide as working section of NAIC Stock Selection Guide & Report.

2.60

30%

3225

200

100
90
80
70
60
50
40
30
25

FIGURE 5-6

164

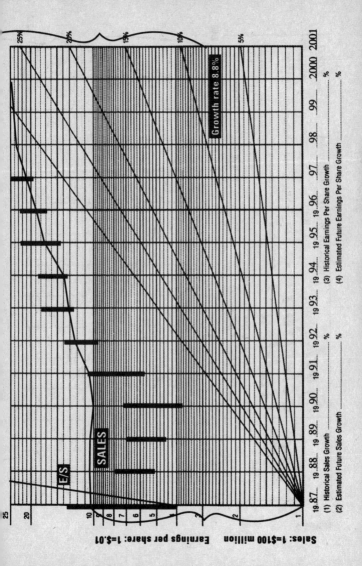

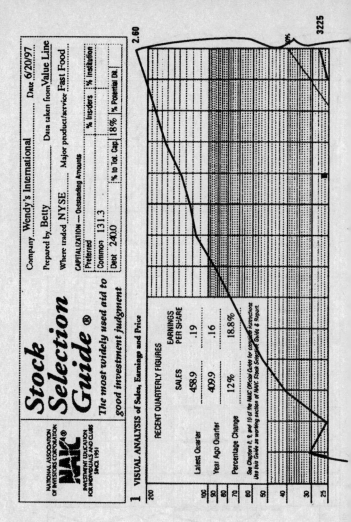

FIGURE 5-7

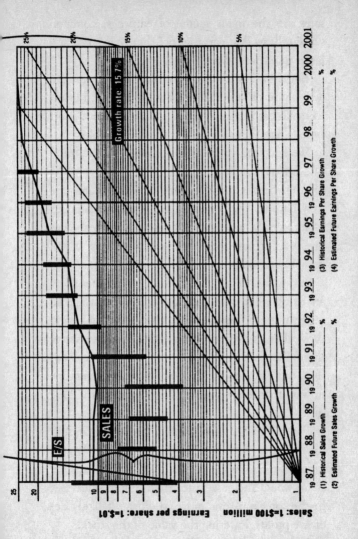

sales are the main source of earnings, common sense tells us that earnings per share can't rise at a faster rate than sales for long.

But they can for a little while. A company can economize on advertising or sell off unused assets to make earnings rise faster than sales for a short time. Then they fall back to the level of sales.

We keep that in mind when we draw the trend line for future earnings per share. If the earnings line has been going up faster than sales lately, as they have for McDonald's (sales grew 8.1 percent, earnings per share 12.6 percent), we make the eps line level off just a little bit in future years. It will probably grow about as fast as sales over time.

As always, we should ask why earnings per share are rising faster than sales. Generally, this would be a sign of good management, and recent figures do show that McDonald's has more sales per server than any other company. Is that the full explanation, or is someone trying to boost the bottom line in ways that don't help the company over the long run?

For example, if Papa's Perfect Pastries began selling off some of its bakeries, it would definitely gain income in the short run. For a while, earnings per share would increase faster than muffin sales. But in the long run, this move would most likely decrease profits, lowering the value of the stock.

In McDonald's case, the earnings per share are

higher, because corporate management has bought back shares of its own company. It's supply and demand: with fewer shares outstanding, the earnings for each share tend to go up. A company often does this when it thinks its shares are undervalued. By creating a relative shortage of shares, it drives the price of each share up.

Diluting the Value

On the other hand, earnings per share will drop if *more* shares are created, diluting the value of each share. If a company with a million shares of stock outstanding suddenly creates and sells a million more, the earnings per share are suddenly half of what they were. This is called a dilution of the value of the stock.

New companies which are growing fast sometimes do get a healthy chunk of their income by selling new stocks—they need that startup money to prime the pump of their business and get profits flowing. However, beware of an older established company that gets too much of its money from stockholders. It's like a young adult whose bank account looks good because he's getting money from his parents. We want our company to be earning the money itself, not depending on an allowance from stockholders.

Sometimes an established company will issue new stock to get money for new factories to meet demand for a product whose sales are going through the roof. That's the best reason of all for issuing new stock. The temporary drop in earnings per share will probably be quickly repaid as more of the product is sold.

Stock Prices

When prices fall, we look to see whether it's in response to genuinely bad news, publicity, a temporary setback, or—as is sometimes the case—the company fails to meet analysts' perceptions. Sometimes we look at this as a buying opportunity.

The stock selection guide tells you pretty clearly whether a stock is in the buy, sell, or hold range. But, as Carnell says, that number isn't "an absolute for elimination."

"Often times, if we really like a company—maybe there are a lot of factors that say it's a good company—but that high price means a lot of other people thought so too. We watch it and if something changes, sometimes even if just the upside down ratio changes to a favorable number, we will buy it."

Price/Earnings Ratio (P/E)

As we've said, by comparing a stock's price to how much the company is making, the P/E ratio tells us whether the stock is worth what we're paying for it.

But with stocks, as with anything else we buy, the law of supply and demand applies. The more people want stocks—as they have in recent years—the more they're willing to pay for a stock of the same value. In a thriving economy and a bull market, the price/earnings ratios of many stocks tend to rise. So how high is too high?

We find out by comparing our stock to others in the same industry. Because some industry's P/Es are naturally higher than others, it makes sense to look at the one we're in. But we also look at where we are in the business cycle. The average P/E of all stocks rises when the economy is good and falls when it's bad. According to NAIC, the average P/E on the Dow Jones Industrials has been as low as 6 and as high as 25 in the last 70 years. Right now it's around 23. That's why, though we originally looked for a P/E of 15 or less, we'll now accept higher P/Es.

Is a relatively high P/E ever acceptable? If a stock's price is expected to keep growing especially fast it can be a judgment call, says Buffy. "You might say, 'Well, this price looks too high to me,' when actually, when you analyze it with the growth potential, it's not." We don't like a P/E to be higher than the company's projected growth rate.

"If the P/E in a stock is going up," says Shirley, "you think, 'Hey, they're not making as much money. What's going on?' You make sure to find out. It's not necessarily bad news. Maybe earnings are dropping because they're out buying another

Stock Comparison Guide

NATIONAL ASSOCIATION
OF INVESTORS CORPORATION

NAIC®

INVESTMENT EDUCATION
FOR INDIVIDUALS AND CLUBS
SINCE 1951

Prepared by _____

Date _____

See Chapter 15 of the *Investors Manual* for complete instructions.

NAME OF COMPANY

GROWTH COMPARISONS
(From Section 1 of the NAIC Stock Selection Guide)

(1) Historical % of Sales Growth						
(2) Projected % of Sales Growth						
(3) Historical % of Earnings Per Share Growth						
(4) Projected % of Earnings Per Share Growth						

MANAGEMENT COMPARISONS
(From Section 2 of the NAIC Stock Selection Guide)

(5) % Profit Margin Before Taxes (2A) Trend (Average for last 5 years)						
(6) % Earned on Equity (2B) Trend (Average for last 5 years)						
(7) % of Common Owned by Management						

PRICE COMPARISONS
(See Sections 3-5 of the NAIC Stock Selection Guide)

(8) Estimated Total Earnings Per Share For Next 5 Years						
(9) Price Range Over Last 5 Years High (3A) Low (3B)						
(10) Present Price						

FIGURE 5-8

172

		(11) Highest	(3D)								
Price Earnings Ratio Range Last 5 Years		(12) Average High	(3D7)								
		(13) Average	(3-8)								
		(14) Average Low	(3E7)								
		(15) Lowest	(3E)								
(16) Current Price Earnings Ratio			(3-9)								
Estimated Price Zones		(17) Lower-Buy	(4C2)								
		(18) Middle-Maybe	(4C3)								
		(19) Upper-Sell	(4C4)								
(20) Present Price Range			(4C5)								
(21) Upside Downside Ratio			(4D)								
(22) Current Yield			(5A)								
(23) Combined Estimated Yield			(5C)								

OTHER COMPARISONS

(24) Number of Common Shares Outstanding			
(25) Potential Dilution from Debentures, Warrants, Options			
(26) Percent Payout	(3G7)		
(27)			
(28)			
(29) Date of Source Material			
(30) Where Traded			

company. It might be something that's perfectly all right. But you always check." But a falling P/E doesn't always mean earnings are up. "The P/E may drop because something causes the stock's price to drop—a lawsuit, or people see in *The Wall Street Journal* that a company had lower earnings than they expected," says Betty. "When Quaker Oats bought Snapple, analysts thought they paid too much for that company and there was a major drop in price. We would have liked to have sold when we first heard the news. By the time we met the price had dropped substantially and we missed our opportunity to sell the stock. We decided to hold the stock until the price came back up." An individual stockholder could have sold at the first sign of trouble.

Final Review

After we've completed all three stock selection guides, we like to line up our most important numbers for each company next to each other so we can compare them. We do this on a one-page sheet called the Stock Comparison Guide (see Figure 5-8 on pages 172–3).

"That page compares these three companies and highlights all the pluses—and minuses—for each one," says Carnell.

Then we get back together and answer all the questions we've just talked about, says Maxine.

"We go back again and really look at what the company has been doing, have they changed management? Are they doing something different? And why are they doing it? We get thoroughly involved."

CHAPTER SIX

How to Read The Wall Street Journal

The Wall Street Journal is required reading for anyone interested in the stock market. It holds a very special place in our hearts because of our own history as an investment club. You could say it was Betty's Aunt Margaret and *The Wall Street Journal* that got us started on our financial journey.

When Aunt Margaret first moved to Beardstown to live closer to Betty, she had all of her money in bank CDs. "In our family there were stories about how so-and-so's father had lost two or three fortunes in the market and the market was a no-no. It was taboo. You didn't even discuss it." Betty explains. With Betty's encouragement, Margaret joined the Beardstown Business and Professional Women's Investment Club and became interested in investing in the market. Betty was a member of the first Stock Study Committee and recalls going to Shirley's house to hunt for potential investments because Shirley subscribed to *The Wall Street Journal* and *Value Line*.

Shirley continues the story, "One night while we were sitting at my kitchen table, I showed Aunt Margaret how to look up a stock in *The Wall Street Journal*. Once she learned how to read the stock tables, she sat there and read them all."

The Journal is a wonderful tool. It reports national and world events from a business perspective, and we think it includes the most comprehensive business news available today. One of the reasons we recommend *The Wall Street Journal* is that, in a single issue, you can view your stock in a larger context. Every day *The Journal* includes a listing of our stocks and most all of the information that we need to keep informed about each stock day to day.

"*The Wall Street Journal* can be bought at any major newsstand. It's not hard to find. It has a lot of good news in it besides the stocks, so it's a very good publication," explains Ann Brewer. "You see an article on widgets and you decide, boy, they're really going to be a hot thing."

As investors, we enjoy reading the articles and analysis. In Section B, there's an index where any company mentioned in that day's edition is listed. Carnell says, "I'm watching McDonald's and Hershey's now for our investment club, so I look them up to see if they're mentioned. If a company is written up in *The Wall Street Journal*, and for some reason it looks interesting, you might want to learn more about it. It's easy to monitor the stocks you have and inspires you to look into other companies."

Ann Corley adds, "If there's a management problem, *The Wall Street Journal* usually says a change is pending or so and so has resigned. It brings you up-to-date a lot of times with the management."

While there is a lot to pick and choose from in this newspaper, our primary information source is Section C of *The Journal*, Money and Investing. This is the section with all those charts and tables, and articles about major indexes. Checking the Money and Investing section is how we keep tabs on our current and future investments.

As the flagship publication of Dow Jones & Company, Inc., *The Journal* is published five days a week. We recommend that you read it every day. Not that we all did before we joined our investment club. Carol recalls, "The investment section used to seem worse than the classifieds. I'd just page through it and wouldn't even look at it. Now, I pay attention to it. My husband even got enthused, and we keep track of stocks we've bought by checking the tables."

Although those little numbers may seem at first like they add up to a big "jumble" to use Carol's word, it's just a matter of learning what they mean to turn them into "can't put it down" reading. By the time you finish this chapter, you will be able to read those stock tables as easily as a recipe in any cookbook. After all, if 80-year-old Aunt Margaret could learn to read *The Journal*, you can too.

When my daughter graduated from Illinois Wesleyan with a degree in economics, she had all A's. One of the things that the college gave her, as a little token her first year out of school, was a year's subscription to The Wall Street Journal. *She was quite thrilled over that.*

—Ann Brewer

Stock Tables

Has this happened to you? You're visiting a friend in another state and he gives you directions to his home. By the time he finishes telling you all the left turns, right turns and important landmarks like the "green house with the crooked shutters," you think you'll never find it.

The first time that someone tried to describe stock tables to us, we felt the same way. Once you understand a few simple points, the stock tables seem less like a complicated set of directions—or indicators—and more like a simple road map that you can follow.

The stock tables published in *The Journal* every day contain information about the price of a stock and how much it gained or lost in value. It also provides clues about the overall health and investment risks of particular companies.

In Section C of any issue of *The Wall Street Journal* is a large, multipage set of tables called the New York Stock Exchange Composite Transactions. (There are also tables for stocks traded on Nasdaq, the American Stock Exchange, and Foreign Stocks.) This is where we watch over most of our stocks. Finding your stock (or stocks) here is easier than locating a box of powdered milk at the supermarket because the stocks are listed by name, in alphabetical order.

Let's take a look at a stock listed in the New York Stock Exchange Composite Transactions table. For this example, we'll choose a stock that most people will recognize, International Business Machines, or IBM. A typical recent IBM stock table listing looks like the following:

| 52 Weeks | | Stock | Sym | Div | Yld % | PE | Vol 100s | Hi | Lo | Close | Net Chg |
Hi	Lo										
109$7/16$	54$11/16$	IBM	IBM	.80	.8	17	46026	104	99$7/8$	99$15/16$	−3$11/16$

This line may look like gibberish to you, but "There's a lot of information," Shirley says, "just in that one little line." The rest of this chapter goes over each of the numbers above, from left to right, so you will be able to decipher the information encoded in these tables.

Annual High and Low Price

Start at the top left-hand side of the stock listings. The first column heading, describing the two numbers to the left of the IBM stock, is 52 Weeks Hi Lo.

The first number tells you, at a glance, the highest price paid for one share of IBM stock during the past 52 weeks, or one year. The next number is the lowest price the stock sold for over the past year. So in our example, during the past 52 weeks, the highest trading price for IBM stock was 109 7/16, which works out to $109.43. The lowest selling price for IBM in the last year was 54 11/16, or $54.68.

Sometimes before the 52 Week Hi number, you'll see a symbol such as an arrow or a lower-case letter. These symbols work like the tiny pictures on a road map, where, for example, a small airplane represents an airport and a heavy red line means a major highway. On stock tables, the little arrow tells you that the stock has set a new high or low price that day. If the arrow points up, it is a 52 week high; if it points down, it is a 52 week low. A small "s" means that the company has had a stock split in the last 52 weeks. A small "a" means extra dividends were issued, and the small "n" means the stock was newly issued within the past year. (Obviously, then, the high and low point covers less than 52 weeks.)

Before you go into a tizzy, thinking you'll never

remember all this, calm down. There is no need to memorize these symbols or even the explanations. When you pick up your *Journal* and see the stock tables, look toward the bottom of the page for something called Explanatory Notes. Just as a road map contains a legend to describe the map's symbols, these notes explain numbers or symbols that accompany a stock's listing. They also provide definitions for the annual high and low price, price earnings ratio, and other stock evaluation measurements.

When we began using *The Journal* for investment information, we constantly referred back to the explanatory notes, just as we constantly check our road maps when we visit somewhere new. You will discover that using the stock tables in *The Journal* is a lot like driving a motor route: after a short while, you won't need maps or written directions to find your way.

After you've studied the stock tables for a while, try quizzing yourself: Open the stock tables and find a stock—any stock. What was its highest trading price last year? Was that a record high? Did the stock split? A few hours ago, you might have been confused. Now, we bet answering those questions is as easy as pie—or maybe easier.

Stock Name Abbreviations and Symbols

The name of the stock follows the 52-week high and low. The column immediately to the right of the high and low is the trading name; the column to the right of the trading name is that stock's abbreviated trading symbol. Let's look at our IBM example again. Symbols may be the same as the company name—as is the case with IBM. Consequently, IBM's name is printed twice because its name is the same as its trading symbol.

Many stock names are easy to recognize: Boeing, the airplane manufacturer, is listed simply as Boeing. Similarly, Disney, the company that has brought us the likes of Mickey Mouse and Snow White, is traded under the name Disney. Other stocks may be trickier to find: Dayton Hudson, the retail department store company is listed under the name DaytnHud. Edify, the company that makes interactive business software such as Electronic Workforce, is traded under the abbreviation EDFY. The symbols for some stocks, such as the car manufacturer Chrysler, are simply a letter. For Chrysler, it's a C. It kind of reminds us of those vanity license plates, like Jimbo 1.

Anyway, if you have any trouble figuring out how a stock is listed in the tables, you can call a broker, call the company itself, or look it up online. (See Chapter Eleven on investing and the internet.)

Dividend

The next column lists the value of the annual dividend (if there is any) that is paid per share every calendar quarter, or every three months. In the IBM example, it is $.80, which means that IBM will pay a dividend of 80 cents per share every year to each shareholder—and it will pay that out in quarterly payments of 20 cents per share. So, for example, if you owned 100 shares of IBM stock, you'd receive $80 in annual dividends, or $20 every three months.

A stock's dividends are a form of profit sharing that the company scoops out of its earnings and pays out to the shareholders. IBM or any other business can change the amount of the dividend paid out, just as you could change the amount of family "profits" that you might give your children as spending money.

The presence or absence of dividends does not always signal a company' s health or its financial woes. However, most people view dividend payments as a sign of health—as well as a form of income. If you owned 1,500 shares of IBM, those 80-cent annual dividends would really add up.

Since our investment club seeks growth, we put all of our cash dividends into a pool of money that we use to invest in more stocks. In some cases you can do that automatically through dividend-reinvestment programs, where any cash dividends on a stock automatically are applied to purchasing more of that company's stock for you. We discuss these DRIPs, as they are called, on page 215 in Chapter Eight.

Yield

In the next column over, the number .8 is the stock's yield. It reveals how much the dividend payment is as a percentage of the stock's selling price. In other words, .8 tells us that IBM investors are getting .8% yield per share on the money invested. You can calculate the yield yourself by dividing the dividend amount by the current price, and then multiplying that by 100. This figure is very important to stockholders who want those cash dividends as income.

We like to use the yield in another way: the yield tells us what the percent of dividend return is on our investment. This can be important if you are choosing between stocks, bonds, certificates of deposit, or other investments.

P/E Ratio

Let's move over: The next number, 17, is the price-earnings ratio that we talked so much about in the previous chapter, one of the most popular evaluation measures of a stock. We use the price-earnings ratio as an attention getter that pulls us in for a closer look, just like that sale on cantaloupes.

The P/E is found by dividing the selling price of the stock by its most recent earnings per share value. IBM's price-earnings ratio of 17 means that the IBM stock price is 17 times the annual earnings per share. As the value of the earnings increases in relation to the selling price of the stock, the price-earnings ratio goes down. A lower price-earnings ratio can mean that you are getting more earnings for your investment dollar than from a stock with a higher ratio. That can be a helpful way of comparing "apples to apples" when you are trying to choose between several different stocks of different values.

A low P/E is a sign that investors don't see much growth from this stock. A high P/E is a sign that the company *currently* doesn't make as much as it may in the future. In other words, investors may be expecting greater earnings growth from a company with a high P/E.

Trading Volume

The listing to the right of IBM's price earnings ratio is 46026, the Vol 100s or trading volume divided by 100. The trading volume tells you the number of shares of that stock that were traded on the day before. To get the actual number, multiply the Vol 100s number, 46026, by 100. Now we see that 4,602,600 shares of IBM stock changed hands in one day.

More than four million shares in a day! When we first saw this number, we thought it was pretty impressive, but we weren't quite sure how it was significant.

A stock with a high trading volume is like that mint-condition grandfather clock that everyone wants to buy for their entry hall—when it comes onto the auction block, a bidding frenzy is sure to follow. You can bet that the grandfather clock will sell for a lot more than the opening bid.

We use the amount of market interest— expressed as the trading volume—in a couple of ways. First of all, many stock investors have a herding instinct and tend to follow the crowd in their buying and selling activities. When the crowds hone in on a stock, the law of supply and demand comes into play: when a stock is increasing in value and is also attracting a lot of investor interest (reflected in a rising trading volume), it is a good sign that the value of that stock will continue to go up.

Those stocks with the highest volume compared with their average volume are usually underlined in the stock tables. The boldface quote lines are those issues with a price change of 5 percent or more from their previous closing.

High volume does not mean a lot of people want to buy that stock: When we see a stock whose price is going down but its volume remains high, we conclude that the "herd" of investors have decided to get rid of this stock. Yes, the stock is attracting a lot of interest, but the price sure is not going up in this case.

Trading volume can also reveal how salable your investment might be. A stock that generates a lot of interest probably will be easy to sell when the time comes to cash in on that investment. Selling a stock that generates low trading volume means that you may have a tough time selling it—just as you would have a tough time selling a pair of ice skates in July at a yard sale on a dead-end street.

Daily High Price, Daily Low Price, and Closing Price

The numbers in the next three columns tell you the highest price one share of a stock sold for the previous day, the lowest price, and the last, or closing, price. In IBM's case, it was a high of $104.50, a low of $99.87, and a final, or closing price of $99.93. These are the most exciting figures to check when you're following a stock. They provide instant gratification or else disappointment, depending on how your stock did that day. Most people can't resist going straight to the closing price and net change to see if they "made" or "lost" money that day. We, of course, try to keep the bigger picture in mind. Also, remember that although you can track the activity of a stock on a daily basis by looking up its closing price in the stock tables, profits or losses are not realized until you actually sell a stock.

If a stock's high and low points are varying greatly, it could be a signal that the stock is on shaky ground and you should be cautious before investing money in it. Since we invest for growth over a five-year period, we are wary of stocks whose value is relatively unstable, or volatile. Other investors who buy and sell on the short term often are attracted to these volatile stocks, hoping to buy at a low point and quickly sell when the stock price momentarily pops up. They are market timers, always trying to dart in and out of the market as fast as sprinters in the 50-yard dash. We're more like marathon runners: slow and steady wins the race.

Net Change

Net change indicates what direction our stock is heading in at the moment—up or down—and how much it has changed in one day.

Net change compares the closing price of the stock today with the closing price of the day before. A minus sign means that the stock went down in value and a plus sign, obviously, means it went up in value. Our IBM example is listed as $-3^{11}/_{16}$. This means that the selling price of IBM stock went down 3.6875 points in the past 24 hours. When there is a significant price change in one day—of 5 percent or more, either up or down—*The Journal* puts the entire quotation in boldface to telegraph the fact that there has been a relatively big change of interest to investors.

If you consistently see plus signs, your stock is headed up in value. However, if you see those alarming minus signs day-in and day-out, the stock is nosing down. Again, what action you take as an investor based on these indicators depends on your personal investing philosophy. It might mean it is time to cut your losses and sell. Or it could mean wait for the price to bottom out before you buy more.

We have been discussing the stock tables of companies listed on the NYSE. There are other tables for stocks traded on Nasdaq, the American Stock Exchange, and foreign exchanges.

Now that you've mastered the stock tables, you're ready to glean even more out of your *Wall Street Journal*. The next chapter will help you understand stock market indexes, a broader way to measure how the market is performing.

CHAPTER SEVEN

How to Read Stock
Market Indexes

How often have you heard a radio or TV broadcaster announcing "Today, the Dow dropped 100 points" or "The Dow hit a record high of 7,860 today." What the heck is the Dow, you wonder, besides a number as fascinating by as a winning lottery number. Hazel used to wonder what this and many other stock terms meant. That's one reason she wanted to join our investment club. Doris says it helps her and all the members to know the terminology.

The Dow Jones Industrial Average is a stock market index. Instead of a single quote for a single stock, an index reflects how several dozen—or several hundred—or several thousand—stocks are faring. This puts your own stock into the context of the larger market, which can give you clues to the prevailing health of the entire market or a particular market sector such as utilities or transportation stocks. Just as stocks are traded on several different exchanges—the New York Stock Exchange, the American Stock Exchange, and Nasdaq—there are a number of market indexes an investor can use.

When stock indexes are looked at over time, they can show you long-term trends in growth or loss for a particular type of stock or for the entire stock market. Investors use graphs of stock market indexes the same way that farmers use long-term weather forecasts.

Stock indexes work the same way: a stock index is a number that has been calculated to reflect the growth or loss of several stock values. Instead of trying to scrutinize one or two stocks, the stock index tells you if the larger market is active and growing or stagnant and shrinking. A good stock index is the weathervane of the market.

Say, for example, you have carefully applied the stock evaluation methods we described in previous chapters to a particular transportation company stock. Several evaluation methods confirm each other, and you have concluded that this stock looks like a winner. Take one more step and look at an index of transportation stocks. If that one transportation stock looks good but the index of most transportation stocks is falling, it might be a good idea to wait until the prices bottom out before buying.

In short, like the farmer's weather forecast, a stock index tells you if the climate of the larger market is right for buying.

Historically, the market indexes worked on a simple principle: Stock market activity increases as the general economy becomes stronger and healthier. Conversely, investment activity in the stock market diminishes in tougher financial times. The rules have been changing, however, with the enormous increase in population represented by baby boomers. Instead of economics, stock market activity has been fueled by demographics: the sheer numbers of middle-aged people now investing through 401k plans, IRAs, and mutual funds have been pushing the market indexes higher and higher.

To reflect the economy more accurately, the various indexes cover different sectors such as utilities, transportation, industry, and technology. Each index reflects how a particular sector is going to perform six to twelve months from now. For example, some domestic manufacturers are facing challenging times as more overseas competitors appear on the horizon. But in computer and electronics, business is very strong as more and more people buy computers, answering machines, fax machines, and the like.

On the other hand, just because say, the semiconductor index is up, doesn't mean a particular semiconductor company's stock is also up. It's not a stock market, so much as a market of stocks.

"Of course, right now the market is up and looks like a lot more fun," Elsie cautions. "There's going to be some times when the market is going to go down, but then you've always got the hope that it's going to go up again." Maxine thinks, because the Dow has been hitting new highs, "It will probably have a correction. But overall in the history of the stock market it has always gone up. Stocks are still the best investment you can make if you get a good portfolio. You can collect stamps, coins, and antiques, but if you collect good stocks, it still has the best return of anything." So don't be scared to look at the Dow Jones or any other index.

The Dow Jones Industrial Average

As far as stock indexes go, the Dow Jones Industrial Average is the best known measure of economic health on the stock market. It was founded in 1884 by Charles Dow, who later founded Dow Jones & Company and *The Wall Street Journal* with his partner, Edward Jones.

Dow's first market measurement was created by taking the average of 11 industrial stocks that, in his estimation, were representative of the nation's economy: they included nine railroads and two manufacturers. By 1896, Dow began regularly publishing his average. One stock of the original 11 still is on the Dow Jones today: General Electric.

The Dow Jones Industrial Average was increased to 30 industrial stocks—and remains so today (although it was trimmed back during the Great Depression of the 1930s).

Today, the Dow Jones Industrial Average is a far cry from that simple average. It actually is adjusted for several factors, such as changes in the representative stocks and stock splits. It is not an average at all, but is truly an index that is designed to express stock market activity and the health of the companies that it represents.

In the business world, if you don't change with the times, you will go the way of the Dodo bird—and the people at Dow Jones know this. Consequently, they have changed this index more than 20 times since its founding in order to keep the Dow as a true representation of the economy. So when we talk about the Dow Jones, we are talking about the latest revision of this old stock market measuring stick.

As you look over the changes to the Dow, it is like viewing an economic history of the last century. Railroads, coal, and oil made the economy run in the late 1800s. Today, the economy runs on silicon computer chips.

The latest change of the represented companies on the Dow Jones Industrial Average occurred in March 1997. As you will see, the changes increased representation of sectors that are growing in importance in today's economy: electronics, finance, and health care. Specifically, computer manufacturer Hewlett-Packard Company went onto the Dow and Texaco Inc. went off. Travelers Group replaced Westinghouse Electric Corp. Johnson & Johnson took the place occupied by Bethlehem Steel, while Wal-Mart Stores Inc. replaced Woolworth Corp.

Prior to this change, three stocks were rotated in 1991. But this four-stock change is the biggest adjustment to the Dow Jones Industrial Average since 1959.

Although the Dow Jones Industrial Average is the best known and probably the most widely quoted stock index in the general media, it is but one of many. Some critics of the Dow Industrial Index say it is not representative of the economy as a whole, but only represents 30 big corporations.

The Dow is expressed as a number—unlike other indexes such as Standard & Poor's 500, which is expressed in dollars. In 1997, the Dow hit the record 8,259 mark.

You may or may not use the Dow as often as we do, but, frankly, we think these different stock indexes all tell us about the same thing if you look at them over time. If there are several years of robust stock market growth—as there has been in the 1990s—you will see the Dow Jones Industrial Average climb. You will also see the Russell 2000, Standard & Poor's, and other indexes climb. And they all will fall when the market takes a tumble as well.

Here are some more of the more widely reported stock market indexes.

Dow Jones Utilities Average

The Dow Jones Utilities Average is set up like the Dow Jones Industrial Average, except that it reflects the activities of 15 utility companies that provide electricity, gas and other energy needs to homeowners and businesses. This index is used by investors to determine the overall strength of utilities.

Dow Jones Transportation Average

This index is similar to the Dow Jones Utilities Average, except that it represents the largest airline, railroad, trucking, and other transportation companies.

The New York Stock Exchange Composite Index

The New York Stock Exchange Composite Index tracks the activities of all of the common stocks traded on the New York Stock Exchange, the world's biggest stock exchange. Common stocks are appropriately named, because they are the most numerous.

The New York Stock Exchange Composite Index actually is one of five indexes maintained by the New York Stock Exchange; these indexes include the industrials, utilities, transportation, and finance stocks. However, the Composite Index is the one most often used by investors because of its wide focus; it doesn't take into account capitalization or specific economic sectors.

Standard & Poor's 500 Index

The Standard & Poor's 500 Index is a popular financial yardstick that is based on a broad foundation of 500 stocks that represent a wide range of capitalization. The capitalization of a company represents the portion of a company's funds that are raised by issuing stocks and bonds. These stocks, with capitalization ranging from $350 million to $160 billion, cover a wide array of market offerings; it includes 400 industrial stocks, 40 utility stocks, 40 financial stocks, and 20 transportation stocks.

As we have said before, the S&P 500 is expressed in dollars. At the time the Dow was hovering around 7,800, the S&P was a tad over $900.

Unlike the Dow Jones index, the S&P 500 includes a system of weighting stocks. Weighting gives more influence to stocks that are viewed as having more of an impact on the economy. As a result, many investors view the S&P 500 as a more accurate index of the general economy's health. We like to look at the S&P 500 as well as the Dow.

The Russell 2000

This index, generated by the Frank Russell company, is calculated from a very large base of 2,000 stocks that are issued by companies that are much smaller than those represented on the Dow. The companies in the Russell 2000 index are considered by investors as small capitalization companies that have an average capitalization of $420 million; its largest companies have a capitalization of about $1 billion. Capitalization describes the company assets that come from issuing stocks and their long-term debt.

The Russell 2000 index is more useful to investors who are looking for smaller stocks that have a strong growth potential.

How to Read the Indexes

Once you know how to read individual stock listings as we described in the last chapter, reading the stock indexes is simple because the technique is almost the same. We have a fast-and-easy way to find the major indexes and it's as close as today's *Wall Street Journal.*

Turn to our well-read Money and Investing, Section C. Now look for a chart called the Stock Market Data Bank. It usually is on page four and it has the day's date listed on top, next to the title.

The Data Bank lists the major indexes:

- *Dow Jones Averages*: Industrials, Transportation, Utilities, Composite, and Global
- *New York Stock Exchange*: Composite, Industrials, Utilities, Transportation, and Finance
- *Standard & Poor's Indexes*: 500 Index Industrials, Utilities, 400 MidCap, 600 SmallCap, and 1500 Index
- *Nasdaq Stock Market*: Composite, Nasdaq 100, Industrials, Insurance, Banks, Computer, and Telecommunications
- *American Stock Exchange Composite*

- *Russell 1000, Russell 2000*, and *Russell 3000*
- *Value-Line*
- *Wilshire 5000*

If you scan along the top row of numbers, it looks like the stock quotes, with columns for daily highs, lows, and closing values, as well several indicators of change.

Here's the Dow Jones Utilities index for one day:

12-Mo		Daily			Net		12-Mo		From	
High	Low	High	Low	Close	Chg	% Chg	Chg	% Chg	12/31	% Chg
240.85	209.47	230.37	227.77	230.37	+1.86	+0.81	+13.49	+6.22	−2.16	−0.93

Look to the headings atop those numbers. Just like in the stock quote, the first two numbers are the high and low points for that index during the past year—only instead of being labeled 52 weeks, they are called 12 months. But a year is a year. Its peak was 240.85 and the low point was 209.47. To the right of that is the title of the index, in this case Utilities.

The following three columns give you a snapshot of the past day's activities, with the highest point reached by the index, the low point, and the value of that index at the close of business: 230.37, the same as the day's high.

To the right of the daily values, you'll see Net Change and % Change. These values are preceded by a plus or minus sign, which indicate if the change is heading up or down. In this example, there is a plus sign, which is expected, because the closing value was the high point of the day. The net change tells you how the closing value listed here compares with the closing value of the previous day. The percent change tells you how much the closing value increased or decreased in one day. In our example, +1.86 means the value increased by 1.86 points over the past 24 hours, which is a .81 percent increase.

To the right of the daily net change and percent change are the same measures over a 12-month period. Comparing the day's change with the year's change gives you an even longer-term sense of how the market is moving. In this example, we see that over the past 12 months, the index rose 13.49 points, representing a 6.22 percent change.

Finally, the last two columns give you the net change and percent change from December 31 of last year (1996, in this case) until today (August 27, 1997 in this case). In this value, we see our first negatives. From 12/31 of last year until today, the utilities index slipped 2.16 points for a decrease of 0.93 percent, suggesting to us that, while the last 12 months saw a 6.22 percent increase, the movement of utility stocks may be slowing—or even beginning a decline. If our individual stocks have peaked, we may want to sell before a longer slide; or if we are in the buying market, we should wait and see if the prices will drop some more before we buy.

Is That Right?

Stock indicators such as trading volume and indexes such as the S&P 500 remind us that in English one word, taken alone and out of context, can have many potential meanings. Take the word "right," for example. Used alone, it can indicate a direction, it can indicate a person's political philosophy, or it can indicate that something is correct.

So remember, if you take something out of context, you risk a bigger chance of misinterpreting its meaning. As you become a more seasoned investor, you will form your own opinions and your favorite stock indexes and stock evaluation methods. Just keep using them all in tandem with each other so that you will not be mislead by a possible misinterpretation of a single number—out of context.

The more information you have, the better your odds of doing well in the stock market. You're equipped to make a better decision.

CHAPTER EIGHT

How to Buy Your Stock

Most of the stocks that are bought and sold by the general public are handled through stockbrokers. But many people are intimidated by the whole world of stockbrokers. As Ann Brewer says, "There's a little fear of hiring a broker if you don't know anyone who has used that broker. I think what holds people back is that fear of perhaps not getting someone you can trust."

There's also plain lack of knowledge. When Carol worked at a manufacturing company, they offered a stock-buying plan in which she participated. When the company moved and she stopped working for it, she thought, "What am I going to do with that stock? I found out it cost me a lot of money to sell it. The bank charged a fee, and then there was the commission, which I didn't understand anything about. I thought, this is a rip-off. I've learned a lot since then."

Our investment club places its investments through our stockbroker, Homer Rieken. We call Homer "our" broker because we have developed an ongoing business relationship into one of trust, respect, and friendship. This is an ideal broker-client relationship; we believe that trust is essential for someone who handles so much of our money and whose investment advice is trustworthy. It is also a pleasure dealing with someone whom we like.

Homer works for a large, full-service stockbrokerage house, A. G. Edwards & Sons. This working relationship is typical for stockbrokers: unlike independent insurance agents, attorneys, or accountants who can work alone, most stockbrokers work for a brokerage house that is a member of one or more stock exchanges. Stock exchanges, such as the New York Stock Exchange or the American Stock Exchange, are the actual places where millions of stocks change hands each day.

This is an important point: you cannot buy or sell stocks on the open market without being a member of a stock exchange. Membership in stock exchanges is extremely limited and that membership is very expensive—that is why even seasoned brokers such as our Homer work for brokerages that are members of one or more stock exchanges.

Choosing a Broker

Your relationship with a stockbroker can be compared to your relationship with a veteran real estate agent who will help you find a home when you move into a new town. You tell your real estate agent what your needs are, how much you can afford to invest in a home, what kind of neighborhood you want. Similarly, when you work with a stockbroker, you tell him what your investment goals are and how much you want to spend and let the broker handle the details of the sale.

The details that a broker handles depends on what sort of firm for which he or she works. Brokers are divided into three major groups: full-service brokers, discount brokers, and deep-discount brokers. These divisions reflect the amount of help—or service—that the brokers provide. Your individual stockbroker may advise you of rising or falling stock prices, alert you to upcoming trends, and tell you what new stocks have good growth potential. In some instances, your broker may simply handle your stock transactions and nothing more. As a result, the fees and commissions that you pay are varied.

Stock in Friendship

When I first tried to find a broker, one didn't want to bother because I was a woman and another one didn't want to bother because I was an artist. (I give away my paintings as gifts or to nonprofit organizations for fundraising.) Eventu-

ally, I found a broker who would deal with an individual woman. That was all right with Homer Rieken. He even bought a painting of mine to benefit a good cause and it hangs in his office today. Last April my children and grandchildren had a birthday and art show for me. Homer flew back from his son's wedding in Hawaii to come to my party. So, you might say that we're friends now.

—Shirley Gross

The realtor makes a commission that is based on the selling price of the house you buy. Stockbrokers make their money by charging commissions for buying and selling stocks. The amount of a stockbroker's commission depends on factors such as the price per share of the stock being purchased and the number of shares being bought. Some brokers charge a flat fee for a purchase—so you would pay, for example, a $25 fee whether you bought 30 shares or 100 shares. These fees vary by broker and even by city, so it is essential that you ask your broker exactly what fees and commissions you will be charged.

For example, we found out that if we bought stock in hundred-share lots, we'd get a better deal from our broker, Doris says. "If we can save a few pennies," she says, "we do."

We look at it this way: If you want the input and advice about individual stocks and trends from in-house professionals, you'll want to go the full-service route. If you feel confident in your research ability, just go to the discount folks to put the trade through. The discount broker offers savings, but leaves the legwork to you, the investor.

Full-Service Brokers

A full-service firm such as A. G. Edwards, Edward D. Jones, or Dean Witter charges a fee starting at less than 1 percent of your stock purchase, and going all the way up to about 5 percent. The fee depends on the selling price of the stock you buy and the number of shares that you buy. Purchases of higher-priced stocks as well as high-volume—many shares at once—tend to have a lower (percent) fee charged—just like it is cheaper to buy your donuts by the dozen. If the full-service firm does a personal financial analysis or does some in-depth tax counseling for you, those additional services could carry fees of several hundred to several thousand dollars.

A good full-service broker should spend a lot of time interviewing *you* before he or she does anything else. Why? Because, in order to serve your investment needs, your broker must know your financial goals, how much risk you are willing to take, what your earnings expectations are, and how much you are willing to invest. In short, the money that you will pay a full-service broker goes toward the advice that the broker and his or her firm offers. Other services include in-house researchers whose job it is to determine overall stock trends and to identify specific investment opportunities that a single broker probably would not have the time to find. These researchers produce detailed reports describing their analysis of different stocks; they share these reports with the firm's stockbrokers and their clients.

As Shirley explains, this is exactly why we use a full-service brokerage. "We don't choose stocks just because somebody downtown said, 'Hey, that's a hot stock, you ought to buy it.' We look it up ourselves. If we don't have it in *Value Line*, we call our broker. If I ask about something that I don't have any material on, he looks it up and he will send us a research sheet. He's very good about it and I always get it the next day."

Some larger full-service brokerages have in-house investment banking divisions, which may provide you with the opportunity to buy a new stock before the rest of the stock market has a chance to buy it and drive up the selling price. Here is how that works: When a company decides to sell its stock to the public for the first time, the release of that first wave of stock shares is called an initial public offering (IPO). Investment bankers play a crucial role when companies decide to issue new stock—especially for an initial public offering.

When those initial stock shares are released, the company does not have the resources to effectively market all of the new shares to the public. Instead, the company relies on investment bankers to take on the task of marketing the stock. Often, the investment banking divisions of several brokerage firms will assume the responsibility of marketing the stock. When those investment bankers assume that responsibility, it is called underwriting the stock release.

If your full-service brokerage is underwriting an initial public offering, you and the firm's other clients might have first crack at the stock. As a result, you could buy the stock at a price that may be lower than when it is driven up by the demand of the general market.

On the other hand, some critics charge that full-service brokers who have investment banking divisions are under pressure to sell the stocks that their investment bankers underwrite. Consequently, some argue, the brokers themselves might push these underwritten stocks more aggressively than another stock that may better suit your personal goals.

Discount Brokers

The federal agency that governs the stock market—the Securities and Exchange Commission—deregulated the price structure for stockbrokers in 1975. Specifically, it did away with minimum set commissions that stockbrokers could charge and opened the market up to competitive pricing. The result of this deregulation is the discount stockbrokerage firm.

Discount brokers can afford to charge less than full-service brokers because they offer fewer services to their clients. Their commission fees typically are affected by the total dollar value of a purchase or sale, or perhaps the number of stock shares purchased, or a sliding scale based on the number of shares and dollar value.

Today, discount firms such as Charles Schwab or Fidelity are flourishing as more confident investors take advantage of the discount brokerage firms' streamlined pricing.

People who choose a discount broker typically do most—if not all—of their own research. Many of these discount clients are seasoned investors who already know the ropes. Others simply are trying to save the money they would pay in the higher commission fees charged by a full-service firm.

Discount brokers do provide some services, but the total shepherding function of a full service broker is absent in a discount house. We have heard of discount brokerage houses offering services such as limited research and access to reports, the ability to trade stocks via the internet, and some investor counseling.

The level of service in many discount firms has been rising due to increased competition between new discount brokers. As competition continues, you can expect to see more discount broker services, such as complete stock reports or newsletters.

HOW MUCH DOES THAT STOCK COST?

This table shows the commissions for 200 shares of IBM and TWA stock.

	Commission ($)
Full-Service (Merrill Lynch)	
IBM	210.00
TWA	78.00
Discount (Charles Schwab)	
IBM	110.00
TWA	58.00
Deep Discount (for IBM or TWA)	
Datek	9.00
E*TRADE	14.95
Ceres Securities	18.00

Deep Discount Brokers

Deep discount brokers are the factory warehouse outlet of the retail stock world. These brokers charge the lowest fees because they simply handle your transactions and do nothing more.

If you look at advertisements in *The Wall Street Journal* or *Money* magazine, you will see that many deep discount brokers encourage their clients to use the internet for their trades—so you don't meet or even talk to the person who handles the trade. It isn't the warmest relationship we've seen, but it can save you a lot of cash over the long run.

Once you are a knowledgeable trader or if you simply want to buy some additional shares of an already proven stock, you may want to consider using a deep discount broker.

As you consider which type of broker to hire, remember this: you are not locked into one type of broker. Many people, including members of our club, use full-service brokers such as Homer Rieken for trades. But we also use discount and deep discount to buy and sell stocks that we have already researched ourselves.

Use different brokers as you would use different tools in your vegetable garden. Each tool, like each type of broker, is best used for certain applications. For example, if you own stock in computer maker Gateway 2000, and you are satisfied with its growth, make your next purchase through a deep discount or discount broker. Why not? You already know what to buy, how much to buy and when to buy.

What You Should Ask a Potential Broker

Say you are hiring a carpenter to put an addition on your garage. One of the first steps you would take would be to check that person's references. You would want the answers to questions such as, "How competent is he?" "Does he do what his clients ask and does he finish on time?" Above all, you'd want to know if the carpenter is trustworthy.

More than likely, you learned about this carpenter from friends and acquaintances who have been satisfied with the carpenter's work. That's common sense, and that's how you should approach any stockbroker you are considering.

The concept of trust is especially important: You will be sharing personal financial information with your broker and you are entrusting your investments with this person as well. Moreover, stockbrokers are not paid according to the success of any stock investments that you place through them. Instead, they are paid by the amount of business they handle—whether it be a percent of the amount you invest or a service charge that is billed to you every time the broker makes a buy or a sale.

Now you have some names of brokers from friends, acquaintances, and, of course, from your Aunt Tillie. Call the broker who you are interested in. See if you are comfortable with this person. Does this broker try to get you to buy some hot tips before finding out about your investment goals? If so, you might want to look elsewhere.

Is this broker willing to take the time to answer your questions, or do you feel that you are being rushed? We believe that our instincts are often accurate. If your first reaction tells you that the broker is not right for you, or if you feel uncomfortable dealing with this person, then it is time to look elsewhere.

Here are some of the questions you will want to ask a potential broker:

What titles and certifications do you have? What relevant education do you have?

What services do you and your firm offer besides handling the buying and selling of stocks? If additional services are offered, do they carry additional charges?

How do you charge your clients, by commissions related to the size of the investment or by set fees?

Do you ever work with professionals in related fields such as accounting or law?

How long have you been a stockbroker? What did you do before you sold stocks?

How long have you been with this brokerage?

These questions are designed to determine the broker's knowledge, experience, attitude, and ethics. If he or she dodges these questions, you should probably begin looking for another broker. Remember, you are entrusting your hard-earned money and personal financial information with this person.

Equally important to asking the broker questions is having the broker interview you. He or she should want to know your specific financial needs. Are you a 28-year-old single person looking for some aggressive growth or are you a 68-year-old married person who is interested in low-risk growth stocks?

Just remember, you are the client—you are hiring the broker. A broker should impress you, not the other way around! Don't be afraid to ask questions.

Do It Yourself: The DRIP Program

No, we are not talking about leaky faucets here: DRIP stands for Dividend Reinvestment Plan.

A dividend reinvestment plan lets you apply your stock dividends toward the purchase of more stock in the same company—automatically. While a dividend reinvestment plan does not suit the short-term stock buyer, it is very useful to people like us who invest in stocks for the long term.

DRIP plans are offered directly by the companies issuing the stock—and this is one of the rare instances where you can bypass a stockbroker. Today, more than 1,000 companies offer DRIP plans, including big companies such as American Express and IBM. The investor may be able to deal directly with the company issuing the stock, thereby bypassing the brokers' commissions (although many companies charge a processing fee to start a DRIP).

We think that the biggest advantage of an investor using a DRIP, though, is that he or she can automatically reinvest the stock dividends into buying more shares of that particular stock, without any additional time or energy. In addition, most DRIPs allow investors to add voluntary cash payments that will be added to the dividends to buy even more shares. You may also sign up for an automatic deduction from your bank account.

One of our friends who opted for a dividend reinvestment plan in a New York utility called Rochester Gas and Electric was puzzled by her stock statement: it noted that she owned 122.56 shares. How can you own a fraction of a share? You can in a DRIP, because as your dividends add up each calendar quarter, they usually do not total the amount needed to buy whole shares. Instead, the dividends add up, like jellybeans in a jar, until the jar is full and another whole share is added. Once you own a stock under a DRIP plan, you can see those fractions of shares grow with each quarterly stock statement that you will receive. We think that this is a wonderful way to introduce our children to the market.

Dollar-Cost Averaging

Still another advantage of a DRIP is that you get the benefit of *dollar-cost averaging*, a stock purchasing technique popular with conservative, long-term investors like us. Dollar-cost averaging means you make regular purchases of a particular stock or set of stocks with a set sum regardless of the market's level. When stock prices dip, you will receive more shares for your money; when stock prices rise, you will receive fewer shares. Over an extended period of time during which stocks have moved both up and down, you find that your average cost per share is lower than the average price for that period. Why? Because you bought more shares when prices were low and fewer shares when prices were high.

Dollar-cost averaging is one of those concepts that is a little tricky to grasp at first, but once you do, you get it for life. Here's how dollar-cost averaging might work:

Date of purchase	Amount invested	Price per share	Number of shares
January 1	$ 500	$10	50
March 1	$ 500	$ 8	62
May 1	$ 500	$ 6	83
July 1	$ 500	$ 5	100
September 1	$ 500	$ 8	62
Totals	$2,500		357

The average *price* per share of this stock is $7.40. But the investor's average *cost* is only $7. This is because when the price was highest, at $10, the investor only bought 50 shares with his $500. When it was lowest, at $5, the investor bought 100 shares. You can see that for this system to work, it requires you to invest on a regular, continuous basis—no matter what.

That's why a DRIP is so effective. The board of directors of a company issuing stock sets its dividends—usually once a year. Say you have 100 shares of stock in Company A. Its board of directors authorizes an annual dividend payment of $1 per share. This means that in a year's time, you will earn $1 per share—even though the stock price goes up and down daily. If you are in a DRIP program, that $1 per share will be applied toward the purchase of more shares of stock. So, if you own 100 shares of Company A, every three months your $25 dividend will purchase you more shares—no matter how much the price of the stock fluctuates. At the end of one quarter, for example, the stock may dip to $91, while the high point may be $102. Your dividends remain constant throughout the year while the stock price goes up and down daily. You wind up buying more stock when the price is low and fewer shares as the price goes up. By year's end, it almost always works out that you have purchased your additional shares at a lower cost than you would have if you had gone out and bought them through a broker.

A DRIP then, over time, creates a snowball effect: each quarter, you own more stock as your dividends are reinvested. Consequently, each quarter, your dividend payments are increased based on your increased ownership—which in turn buys additional shares even faster. It's like the principle of compound interest: your money makes you more money.

It is easy to find out if a particular company offers a DRIP. Several financial firms, such as Standard & Poor's, publish directories of companies offering dividend reinvestment plans. You probably can find these directories in your public library and buy directly by contacting the company's shareholder's relations department.

If you already own stock that you wish to keep for growth, check with the company's shareholder relations department to see if that company offers its stockholders a dividend reinvestment plan. If it does, you can set up a DRIP through that office.

We think that DRIP plans are great for small investors as well as large investors. And they are easy: once you've started your DRIP, all you have to do is monitor that stock's health on the stock tables. As long as it grows and consistently issues dividends, you can keep the DRIP going.

The NAIC DRIP

One very easy way to get started in a dividend reinvestment program is to enroll in the low cost investment plan sponsored by the nonprofit National Association of Investors Corporation (NAIC). Once you are a member, you can start your DRIP by buying one or more shares of stock from any of the companies that participate in the NAIC program. Participating companies cover many industry sectors and include businesses such as Dana, Diebold, RPM, Pepsico, Mobil, Century Telephone, Intel, and dozens more. Members receive listings of participating companies, or they can be viewed on the NAIC website at www. better-investing.org.

Ann Brewer says she invests in several companies with a DRIP. "I put a hundred dollars a month in, just like a bill," she says. "I got set up through the NAIC because I am a member. For a new investor, that's a good way to start. You're saving a brokerage fee.

"If you go through NAIC, there's an entire page that has over 150 companies that participate. The only thing that might be a little detriment is there is a time delay before the first trade is made. You send your money and they establish your account in whichever company you choose. For instance if you're going to invest in Intel, you look in the paper and see the stock's selling at 47, then you add a $10 fluctuation charge, plus a $7 first-time setup fee and they buy the first share of stock. After that, you deal directly with the company. They send you a quarterly report so you know how many shares you have, current market price, and the amount of the dividend."

The actual purchase is easy: all you have to do is fill out the Low Cost Investment Program enrollment form and send to the NAIC by mail, e-mail, or even by telephone. Enrollment forms can be ordered over the telephone or they can be downloaded from the NAIC website. The purchase is made directly through NAIC. Your only cost besides the stock is a $7 one-time startup charge for your DRIP account and a fluctuation fee, which is $10 per company or per share.

To join NAIC and to order DRIP enrollment forms, contact NAIC Customer Service at (248) 583-6242, or FAX (248) 583-4880. Those who are online can e-mail NAIC customer service at: service@better-investing.org. Of course, you don't have to go through NAIC. Carol reminds us. "You can go to the library and find a book on DRIPs. Some companies offer direct purchases."

Choosing a Financial Planner

Financial planners are paid to look at your big picture. It is their job to thoroughly assess your financial goals and your financial resources. From that information, a financial planner will set up a long-range program for you to follow. Like a recipe, your financial plan will involve taking a cup of this— perhaps a mutual fund—and a teaspoon of that—

maybe a savings bond—to create a satisfying financial pie.

Personal financial goals for one person are completely different from those of another person. It is a financial planner's job to apply the general rules and financial facts-of-life to match each individual client's circumstances.

You will most likely want to have a financial planner if you are a serious investor. Your planner will coordinate your financial goals with the complex realities of the stock market, insurance law, economic trends, and changes in tax legislation.

Be sure your financial planner has some kind of formal training. Your planner should be someone with a strong financial background. Your financial planner will chart much of your economic future; don't leave it in the hands of an amateur.

To choose your financial planner, follow the same logic you do in choosing a stockbroker: first, identify potential planners from friends, business associates, relatives, or through advertisements and literature. Set up a personal interview with this planner. Learn about his or her educational and professional background and ask for a list of references.

Most competent financial planners come from a fiscal or legal background, having professional training and experience in accounting, banking or finance, insurance, stocks and securities, or tax law. In many cases, their titles reveal their specialties.

Some common titles that financial planners use include CFP (certified financial planner), CPA (certified public accountant), or a CLU (chartered life underwriter, an insurance specialist). A Chartered Financial Consultant (ChFC) typically comes from an insurance background. A ChFC, while primarily insurance-oriented, has a broader base in financial planning training. Most planners, both commission- and fee-based, are accredited. Regardless of the certification, keep in mind that the level of expertise and quality of service varies. You'll find a description of certifications and the institutions that award them below.

Above all, make sure you feel comfortable with this person. If you are not comfortable, move on to another planner.

FINANCIAL PLANNERS: WHAT'S IN A NAME?

Accredited Estate Planner (AEP): *Awarded to financial planners who pass an exam administered by the National Association of Estate Planners and Counselors in Bryn Mawr, Pennsylvania.*

Chartered Financial Analyst (CFA): *Before being certified by the Association for Investment Management and Research (AIMR) in Char-*

lottesville, Virginia, a chartered financial analyst must have three years experience in stock analysis and money management, pass three exams administered by the AIMR, and agree to adhere to the AIMR code of professional and ethical standards.

Certified Financial Planner (CFP): A Certified Financial Planner must have a bachelor's degree plus three years of financial planning–related experience, in addition to completing courses of study at a college or university that offers a financial planning curriculum, and pass a certification examination administered by the Certified Financial Planner Board of Standards in Denver, Colorado. CFPs must also complete thirty hours of continuing education every two years and sign an annual disclosure statement regarding ethical conduct.

Certified Fund Specialist (CFS): A CFS specializes in stocks and mutual funds. Candidates must complete a six-month course and pass a mutual fund examination administered by the Institute of Business and Finance in La Jolla, California. The Institute also offers other certifications, requiring varying lengths of study, including Board Certified for Mutual Funds (BCM), Board Certified for Estate Planning (BCE), Board Certified for Securities (BCS), Board Certified for Income Taxes (BCT), and Board Certified for Insurance (BCI).

Chartered Life Underwriter (CLU): The American College in Bryn Mawr, Pennsylvania, awards this professional designation to candidates who have three years of business experience, agree to comply with the College's Code of Ethics and procedures, and who pass a ten-course curriculum that includes estate planning, financial planning, group benefits, income taxes, investments, life insurance, and retirement planning.

Chartered Financial Consultant (ChFC): This designation is awarded by the American College to candidates who have already earned the Chartered Life Underwriter certification and who pass three additional courses: financial decision-making at retirement, financial planning applications, and wealth accumulation planning.

Chartered Mutual Fund Consultant (CMFC): Chartered Mutual Fund Consultants must take a nine-module home-study course, pass a proctored final exam, and sign a code of ethics administered by the National Endowment for Financial Education in Denver, Colorado, and the Investment Company Institute in Washington, D.C.

Certified Public Accountant (CPA): To earn a CPA designation, a candidate must pass a national examination and also be certified in the state in which he practices. CPAs specialize in accounting and state and federal tax laws.

Enrolled Agent (EA): *Enrolled agents are tax preparers who have passed an exam administered by the Internal Revenue Service and who maintain their credentials through continuing education. EAs are authorized to represent clients at IRS audits.*

National Association of Financial and Estate Planning Certified Estate Advisor (NCEA): *Awarded to individuals who complete NAFEP training and pass a test administered by NAFEP, based in Salt Lake City, Utah. Successful candidates possess the skills and knowledge to assist clients with trust planning.*

Personal Financial Specialist (PFS): *A PFS is an accreditation awarded to CPAs who are members of the American Institute of Certified Public Accountants (AICPA) and who have a college education in accounting and finance, on-the-job training under a CPA's supervision, and who have passed an exam administered by the AICPA. A PFS must also comply with State Board of Accountancy regulations and adhere to the AICPA's Code of Professional Conduct.*

Registered Financial Consultant (RFC): *The International Association of Registered Financial Consultants in St. Louis, Missouri, awards this certification to candidates who complete the IARFC training program and pass exams.*

> **Registered Investment Advisor (RIA):** An RIA has registered with state securities regulators and is qualified to give investment advice.

Fees for Financial Planning

You may find that a financial planner can provide valuable advice and guidance in managing your portfolio. They work on three different types of fee structures: commission-based, hourly fee-based, and per project. Commission-based planners will offer direction and then sell stocks. Payment for their services is in the form of a commission on the sale of the securities. Fee-based planners do not sell stocks, but bill clients on an hourly or project basis. According to a 1997 survey conducted by the National Endowment for Financial Education the media hourly fee is $100. Commissions could range from 1 percent range of assets under management to 5 percent per transaction. Single consultations, according to the American Institute of Certified Financial Planners Board of Standards, range from $500 to $10,000 depending on the project.

Many people prefer fee-based planners because they believe that commission-based planners' advice could be influenced by the lure of more commissions.

Learn how your financial planner charges for his or her services. Some financial planners charge a combination of fees and commissions. Obtain a written estimate or a schedule of the fees that you will have to pay. If your planner acts on your behalf to buy insurance or bonds, you can try asking that the commission be rebated to you, or counted against your fees.

What to Ask a Financial Planner

Here are some questions that one might use to quiz a financial planner:

What credentials and relevant courses and degrees do you have?

Do you charge by fee, by commission, or a by combination of the two? Before I hire you, I will need a printed schedule of all the fees and charges that I will be expected to pay.

How would you describe your experience working in the field of finance and financial planning? What attracted you to work as a financial planner?

How does your past experience help your role as a financial planner?

Are most of your clients private individuals such as myself, or are they businesses or large groups?

Do you coordinate your efforts with accountants, tax attorneys and other professionals in related fields?

If I hire you, would you be willing to coordinate

my financial planning with my personal attorney and accountant?

The services provided by stockbrokers and financial planners can be invaluable. Use the information in this chapter to evaluate stockbrokers and financial planners with the same scrutiny as you evaluate individual stocks. In our experience, the time you spend in such evaluations will pay you back—with interest.

CHAPTER NINE

How to Read an Annual Report

Publicly held companies try to put their best foot forward every year in a public relations exercise called the annual report—a magazine length, slickly produced booklet that is distributed to shareholders, the media, and any other interested person.

Corporations are always willing to send their annual reports, Carol says, if you just write to them and ask. "Understanding the report takes a little more effort," she adds. They are usually issued about three months after a company's fiscal year ends. If a company's fiscal year closed in December, for example, its 1998 annual report would be available in March 1999.

Watching the stock in the months and years after you buy it is an important part of doing your homework. And so is checking it out thoroughly before you buy. As Doris says, "One unique thing about the Beardstown Ladies' method is the way we follow our stocks at each monthly meeting with our own brand of portfolio management.

"The annual report is part of our process for watching stocks that we own. Within the club, we are each assigned stocks to watch. The financial partner sees that whoever's watching it gets that company's annual report. We buy these stocks to hold, but we don't buy them to forget."

"Annual reports used to be black and white and all figures. Now they have all their products listed and pictures in color. They're fun to read," Hazel says. In fact, at a seminar on reading annual reports, Margaret heard that you can tell about the financial condition of a company by looking at the graphics and the cover of the report. If it's pretty and professionally done, the company is probably doing all right.

Well, as Elsie points out, you never see a company that talks against itself in an annual report. "We take a more logical approach and look at the bottom line," she says. How do you calculate the bottom line, though, from all those numbers? In this chapter we'll show you how to do that.

Learning to read an annual report is like going on a scavenger hunt or breaking a secret code. Once you know how to do it, it offers all sorts of treasures. Most annual reports begin with a letter to shareholders from the chief executive officer of the company. The CEO generally reviews the past year, citing highlights, explaining difficulties, and laying out the plans for the next year of more. If a company had a difficult year, check how much candor the CEO uses in his letter and how thoughtfully any strategy for the future is explained. If, on the other hand, past problems are glossed over without any suggestions for how to reverse them, you might be wary.

While there are no federal rules governing the content of these letters, they illustrate the CEOs impression of the past year's activities. Some CEOs tend to gloss over problems or shortfalls, while some are candid and blunt. We favor the latter: as shareholders, we don't want to read public relations fluff; we want the hard news about our investments!

The rest of the text will most likely discuss the company's operations in general terms, mentioning major accomplishments such as discoveries, new products, acquisitions, and the like. From this information, you can discern what aspects of its business the company views as significant.

Most important to potential or current investors, however, are the financial charts, which tell a more objective story. The Securities and Exchange commission regulations require that annual reports contain certain standard financial information. The company's descriptions of its operations and strategies in the text and the numbers in the financial charts can provide some really valuable insight.

These numbers are generally audited by a reputable accounting firm. Take the time to read the auditor's opinion, which should include a standard endorsement of the figures, stating that they are "presented fairly . . . in conformity with general accepted accounting principles." If there is any departure from such language, read it carefully—it may mean a problem.

"If something in the report raises a question or a red flag, sometimes if you read the footnotes, that may answer your questions. If it doesn't that may tell you something too," says Carnell. "Judgment plays a part. Do you really buy that explanation or not?"

HOW TO FIND AN ANNUAL REPORT

You can order annual reports by telephone, by mail, or through the internet (most companies have their own websites). Companies that are on line often post their annual reports on their websites—enabling you to download the report right into your home computer in a matter of minutes instead of waiting for a week for the report to arrive in the mail. Your stockbroker can give you the telephone number, address, or website of the company that you have in mind. More likely than not, your company has a toll-free number, which you can find by dialing the national toll-free di-

rectory at 1-800-555-1212. If you are logged on to the internet, you can find your company's website through the search engines on your internet browser software. Also, Value Line lists the company address and telephone number in the right-hand, midsection of each sheet.

Balance Sheet

The balance sheet of your annual report is the first stop in a review of your stock's well being. There are hundreds of numbers on the balance sheet, which can include corporate records that go back for several years.

Don't be intimidated by the numbers on the balance sheet. The numbers can be divided into three major categories: assets, liabilities, and shareholders' equity. Assets indicate what the company owns and include cash, buildings, office equipment, and inventory. Liabilities indicate what a company owes and include bills, long-term debts, and, of course, taxes. Shareholders' equity is the value of the stockholders' share of the business, which is the excess of assets over liabilities. In other words, the assets always equal—or *balance*—liabilities plus shareholders' equity.

Assets are divided into several subcategories. Current assets refers to assets that a company expects will be converted into cash within a year.

Current assets, which include cash and cash equivalents, is one of the most important lines on the balance sheet. It tells you how much cash the company has on hand.

The next two lines in the assets category are accounts receivable and inventories. These items are listed as assets because they could be converted to cash.

Accounts receivable (sometimes simply called receivables) is the money owed the company for goods it has already sold to customers. Items put on lay-away, payments from banks for check and credit card purchases, are examples of receivables.

Inventories are the unsold finished goods, work in progress, and raw materials that a company has on hand but that have not been sold. Beware of large inventory, which might indicate the company's product isn't selling as well as it should.

Net property is calculated by taking all of the buildings, land, and equipment owned by the company and subtracting their depreciation. If you've ever bought a new car, you know exactly what depreciation is: the value of a product begins to diminish after the sale as the product becomes older and more worn out. Companies take this diminished value into account by subtracting the accumulated depreciation of their holdings from their assets to reach the value of their net property.

To summarize: Current assets plus net property, plant, and equipment equal total assets.

Current liabilities are debts that are due within a year. Think of total current liabilities as that pile of household bills that sits on your desk at home. Accounts payable are debts owed to creditors for items such as materials, supplies, and services. Also included under current liabilities are debts to lenders that are due within a year, lease obligations, and income taxes.

A company's long-term debt refers to mortgages, bonds, and other long-term loans that have been secured by the company. These types of loans are essential for an expanding business, but it is important to keep these debts under control. If, for example, a company's long-term debt is growing at a faster rate than its revenues, it could mean that the company is borrowing money to stay afloat.

To summarize: Current liabilities plus long term debt equal total liabilities.

Shareholders' equity indicates how many shares of preferred and common stock are outstanding. Preferred shares are listed first because they have a prior claim before common shareholders to dividends and assets. Should a company go out of business, for example, common shareholders will be paid only after all bondholders and preferred shareholders are compensated.

Another important line item is called retained earnings. Retained earnings refer to the amount that the company reserves for the growth of the business before paying dividends to shareholders.

It is an important number because it tells you the amount of the company's earnings from sales that have been reinvested in the company. New companies typically do not pay dividends to their stockholders, but instead they plow as much money as possible back into the company itself. Don't be misled by the fact that retained earnings are listed under liabilities: unlike other payments out, they go right back into the company.

Since we invest for growth, we interpret a steady retained earnings as a positive sign that the company is investing in itself. Stocks that have high retained earnings while still holding a large and growing amount of cash (under assets) can be a good bet, especially if their long-term debt is diminishing.

Analyzing the Balance Sheet: A Case Study

We first studied the discount retailer Wal-Mart after Shirley noticed that the parking lots of Wal-Mart stores were always full and customers were buying. Look at the balance sheet from Wal-Mart's 1996 annual report (see Figure 9-1 on pages 238–9). At the top, you'll see in parentheses *amounts in millions*. This is simply to save space. The number 6 on the chart, for example, means six million; the number 100 means 100 million. Below *amounts in millions* is a date: January 31. This date is the end of Wal-Mart's fiscal year. While most companies end their fiscal year on December 31, Wal-Mart

FIGURE 9-1
Wal-Mart Annual Report

CONSOLIDATED BALANCE SHEETS

(Amounts in millions)

January 31	1997	1996
Assets		
Current Assets:		
Cash and cash equivalents	$ 883	$ 83
Receivables	845	853
Inventories		
At replacement cost	16,193	16,300
Less LIFO reserve	296	311
Inventories at LIFO cost	15,897	15,989
Prepaid expenses and other	368	406
Total Current Assets	17,993	17,331
Property, Plant and Equipment, at Cost:		
Land	3,689	3,559
Building and improvements	12,724	11,290
Fixtures and equipment	6,390	5,665
Transportation equipment	379	336
	23,182	20,850
Less accumulated depreciation	4,849	3,752
Net property, plant and equipment	18,333	17,098
Property under capital lease	2,782	2,476
Less accumulated amortization	791	680
Net property under capital leases	1,991	1,796
Other Assets and Deferred Charges	1,287	1,316
Total Assets	$39,604	$37,541

CONSOLIDATED BALANCE SHEETS (cont.)

(Amounts in millions)

January 31	1997	1996
Liabilities and Shareholders' Equity		
Current Liabilities:		
Commercial paper	$ —	$ 2,458
Accounts payable	7,628	6,442
Accrued liabilities	2,413	2,091
Accrued income taxes	298	123
Long-term debt due within one year	523	271
Obligations under capital leases due within one year	95	69
Total Current Liabilities	10,957	11,454
Long-Term Debt	7,709	8,508
Long-Term Obligations Under Capital Leases	2,307	2,092
Deferred Income Taxes and Other	463	400
Minority Interest	1,025	331
Shareholders' Equity		
Preferred stock ($.10 par value; 100 shares authorized, none issued)		
Common stock ($.10 par value; 5,500 shares authorized, 2,285 and 2,293 issued and outstanding in 1997 and 996, respectively)	228	229
Capital in excess of par value	547	545
Retained earnings	16,768	14,394
Foreign currency translation adjustment	(400)	(412)
Total Shareholders' Equity	17,143	14,756
Total Liabilities and Shareholders' Equity	$39,604	$37,541

and many other retailers end their fiscal years a month later, presumably to give them time to produce their year-end tabulations after the Christmas season's rush of business. Therefore, the 1997 Wal-Mart annual report illustrates the business that occurred from January 31, 1996, through January 31, 1997.

So, starting at the beginning of Wal-Mart's balance sheet, you'll see under Assets that the company has $883 in cash. Remember, that's 883 *million* dollars! Having that much cash on hand is important; it will carry the company through periods of slack sales or through unexpected expenses.

Wal-Mart lists $845 million in receivables. For a company such as Wal-Mart, accounts receivable come from thousands and thousands of retail customers. For a smaller company with a handful of clients, a large accounts receivable could be a danger sign: If one large debtor goes out of business, the company could lose a large chunk of its assets.

For a retailer such as Wal-Mart, current assets include inventory. Wal-Mart's inventory, which includes all of the things you see lining the shelves in a Wal-Mart store waiting to be sold, is $16,193 million. On the balance sheet, the total current assets is $17,993 million.

The following several lines on the Wal-Mart annual report list land, buildings and other properties which all add up to Net Property. For Wal-Mart, the value of its net property, plant and equipment is $18,333 million. Miscellaneous other assets total $3,278 million. So then, Wal-Mart's total assets—the sum of everything it owns—is total current assets ($17,993 million) plus net property ($18,333 million) plus miscellaneous assets ($3,278), which adds up to $39,604 million on its 1997 report.

Now that we know what Wal-Mart owns, let's see what Wal-Mart owes. Look down the page until you find Liabilities and Shareholders' Equity.

The first number to look for in the liability category is the accounts payable, which refers to the money that Wal-Mart owes other companies for supplies and equipment. Wal-Mart owes $7.628 billion. The next line, accrued liabilities, is $2.413 billion; this is the money that Wal-Mart has to spend for employee salaries and other short-term, anticipated expenses.

Accrued income taxes, the next line on the balance sheet, is, of course, the money Wal-Mart owes the government: $298 million.

Long-term debt due within one year, $523 million, is listed on the next line of Wal-Mart's report. Next is obligations under capital leases due within one year. This figure, which totals $95 million, refers to money that Wal-Mart has to pay in the next year for property that it leases.

Total current liabilities, the next line, is the debt that Wal-Mart must pay during the next year: $10,957 million.

Long-term debt for 1997 is $7,709 million. If

you check Wal-Mart's 11-Year Financial Summary table in the annual report, you will find that the long-term debt has been rising since 1987 until it peaked at $8.5 billion in 1996. Normally, we would be alarmed with an increasing debt, but Wal-Mart has been a rapidly expanding company over the past decade, and its long-term debt has risen accordingly as it added new stores and inventories. The dip in debt between 1996 and 1997 is a healthy sign that Wal-Mart is getting its long-term debts under control. We will watch this figure carefully: as stockholders, we want to see Wal-Mart's long-term debt continue to subside.

Total shareholders' equity in Wal-Mart is listed as $17,143 million. That's how much of its business is owned by the stockholders.

Note that Wal-Mart's retained earnings increased from $14,394 million in 1996 to $16,768 million in 1997. It is a healthy sign to see that Wal-Mart's long-term debt is diminishing and its retained earnings level is on the increase. These are two trends that we like to see: getting debt under control while plowing more money into our company. Both of these will strengthen a business in the long run and make the stock a better investment over the long haul.

To check whether or not Wal-Mart's balance sheet is "balanced," add shareholders' equity to the total liabilities and the answer should equal total assets. On Wal-Mart's consolidated balance sheets, total current liabilities ($10,957 million) plus long-term debt ($7,709 million) plus long-term obligations under capital leases ($2,307 million) plus deferred income taxes ($463 million) plus minority interest ($1,025 million) plus total shareholders' equity ($17,143 million) is $39,604 million.

What do you know? Total assets is also $39,604 million.

Income Statement

The income statement is a way to measure a company's profitability over time. At the top of the statement is the figure for net sales, the amount of money collected for all goods or services sold minus returns and allowances. Underneath net sales will be a list of the operating costs and expenses, which many include cost of goods sold, marketing and administrative expenses, research and development, and other expenses. Subtract operating costs and expenses from net sales and the result will be operating income. To calculate net income—also known as the bottom line because it actually comes at the bottom of the chart—operating income is added to other income minus taxes. The bottom line is important to shareholders because this is the source of dividend payments.

Net income is a very good way of deciding how a company is really doing. If a company's sales are going up from year to year, but those sales are not keeping pace with expenses, the company will be headed for troublesome cash flow problems. Since net income takes expenses into account, a steadily increasing net income shows that sales and other income are outpacing the cost of doing business—which is the way a healthy company should operate.

To measure inventory turnover, divide the cost of goods sold by the total inventory figure on the balance sheet. If the costs of good sold is $1 million and the inventory is $250,000, the inventory turnover is four times. Generally, the higher the turnover the better, but you should compare this figure with those of competitors, because norms vary by industry.

Plant turnover is another useful ratio: net sales divided by the amount spent for property, plant, and equipment, listed on the balance sheet. Again the higher the better and it should increase over time. If a company increases its expenditures without growing sales, it's possible that its assets are not being used efficiently.

You can calculate profit margin using numbers from the income statement. Profit margin is one figure that we always keep track of on our stock reports. The profit margin of a company is most useful when it is tracked over several years. An increasing profit margin is a sign of a stock with healthy growth prospects while a decreasing profit margin is a cause for concern. Divide profit before taxes by net sales to determine profit margin. If the profit margin is rising, management may be cutting costs successfully. The text may give you clues as to whether or not a company plans further cost reductions, which is good for profitability.

To determine return on equity, you need to look at both the balance sheet and the income statement. Divide net income by book value. Book value is the value of common stock plus retained earning plus surplus reserves (sometimes referred to as something else such as *capital in excess of par value*), all figures that can be found on the balance sheet.

Finally, you may want to calculate sales per employee. Simply divide net sales by the number of employees, which you should be able to find somewhere in the annual report. With both return on equity and sales per employee, the higher the ratio the better. Even more important, however, is growth over time and better performance than competitors.

The Income Statement: A Case Study

Now look at Wal-Mart's Consolidated Statements of Income (Figure 9-2 on page 246).

Net sales, the first figure under revenues, totals $104,859 million for Wal-Mart in 1997. Net sales is the money that Wal-Mart took into its cash registers (minus any merchandise that was returned). A healthy company should have its net sales level increasing year to year, and this has been the case

FIGURE 9-2
Wal-Mart Annual Report

CONSOLIDATED STATEMENTS OF INCOME

(Amounts in millions except per share data)

Fiscal years ended January 31,	1997	1996	1995
Revenues:			
Net sales	$104,859	$93,627	$82,494
Other income-net	1,287	1,122	918
	106,146	94,749	83,412
Costs and Expenses:			
Cost of sales	83,663	74,654	65,586
Operating, selling and general and administrative expenses	16,788	14,951	12,858
Interest Costs:			
Debt	629	692	520
Capital leases	216	196	186
	101,296	90,403	79,150
Income Before Income Taxes	4,850	4,346	4,262
Provision for Income Taxes			
Current	1,974	1,530	1,572
Deferred	(180)	76	9
	1,794	1,606	1,581
Net Income	$ 3,056	$ 2,740	$ 2,681
Net Income Per Share	$1,33	$1.19	$1.17

for Wal-Mart. Over the past four years, Wal-Mart's net sales increased from $67.3 billion in 1994 to $82.5 billion in 1995, $93.6 billion in 1996 to $104.9 billion in 1997. Other income is $1,287 million. This might be money generated by accrued interest, consulting fees, or services not related to the company's primary product line.

The next two lines, under costs and expenses, tells us how much of Wal-Mart's revenues are spent on doing business. Cost of sales is $83,663 million, while operating, selling, and general and administrative expenses is $16,788 million. Interest costs total $845 million.

When all of Wal-Mart's expenses ($101,296 million) are subtracted from all of its sales ($106,146) the income totals $4,850 million. But that's before taxes. Once they are subtracted, the final net income for Wal-Mart in 1997 is $3,056 million.

Looking at the Consolidated Statements of Income table, note that Wal-Mart's net income grew from $2.6 billion in 1995 to $2.7 billion in 1996 and up to the $3.05 billion mark for 1997. As Wal-Mart stockholders, we are gratified to find that Wal-Mart's net income continues to grow—another sign of a healthy stock.

At the bottom of the company's income sheet, you will find a net income per share of $1.33. Income per share, which is also called earnings per share, is another measure of the company's profitability. You want to buy a stock from a company whose income per share steadily rises from year to year. Wal-Mart's net income per share has risen from $1.17 in 1995 to $1.19 in 1996 and to $1.33 in 1997.

To calculate Wal-Mart's profit margin we divide the net income figure on the financial summary for 1997, $3,056 million, by the net sales, $104,859 million, to get 0.029. Multiply 0.029 by 100 to get the answer in percent, which is a profit margin of 2.9 percent.

Our Wal-Mart stock's profit margin has been decreasing: In 1990, for example, the profit margin was 4.1 percent. In 1993, the profit margin fell to 3.6 percent, to 3.5 percent in 1994, and to 3.2 percent in 1995. It has held steady at 2.9 percent in 1996 and 1997. We are going to watch this margin carefully.

Return on shareholders' equity is listed in the Wal-Mart report under its 11-Year Financial Summary at 19.2 percent for 1997. Return on equity can also be calculated by dividing the net income on the income sheet with the stock's book value. The larger the return on equity, the healthier the company.

Sales per employee is the final calculation we make based on information in our financial reports. This number is reached by dividing the net sales ($104,859 million) by the number of employees found elsewhere in the report (728,000). The result is that Wal-Mart has $144,037 in sales per employee. Over time, sales-per-employee number should grow, as it has with Wal-Mart. A growing sales-per-employee number means that the company is not overstaffed and the work force is productive.

Now that we have all of this information, let's put it together to review our Wal-Mart stock:

Net sales: Wal-Mart took in $104.8 billion in sales for 1997, and its sales level has consistently grown by double digits, year to year, for the past decade. This is a healthy sign. However, the 11-Year Financial Summary in the report indicates that Wal-Mart's net sales increased 13 percent last year and 12 percent in 1997. But between 1987 and 1995, the annual growth in Wal-Mart's net sales never dipped below 20 percent. In fact, the annual growth rate in sales has steadily diminished since 1987, when it was 41 percent. Although total sales are increasing steadily year to year, the rate of sales growth has slowed. Why? There could be several answers: perhaps Wal-Mart is facing tougher competitors. Maybe Wal-Mart is approaching a saturation point in its market. (To date, Wal-Mart has at least 1,960 stores in the United States.)

Sales per employee: The 1997 annual sales per employee for Wal-Mart is $144,037. The sales per employee level at Wal-Mart has showed a steady increase over the past three years: It was $132,627 in 1995; $138,706 in 1996 and $144,037 in 1997. This increasing sales per employee level is another sign of a healthy cash flow. As the level of sales increases faster than the number of employees, we can be further assured that management is successfully boosting profitability and controlling costs.

Net income: While the total sales growth rate is slowing, Wal-Mart's net income still outpaces its operating expenses. This is a good sign.

Return on shareholders' equity: At a healthy 19.2 percent, it is steadily diminishing every year. This is a situation that we will continue to watch, but we do not think it is serious. When this slowing return is taken in the context of many more positive indicators such as increasing sales, increasing net income, and increasing sales per employee, we do not consider it to be a critical problem.

Long-term debt: After steadily increasing since 1989, it peaked in 1996 at $8.5 billion. In 1997, Wal-Mart's long term debt was down to $7.7 billion. The previous growth of long-term debt reflects Wal-Mart's huge investment in expansion. Between 1989 and 1997, the number of Wal-Mart stores climbed from 1,259 to 1,960 stores; its major stores, called Domestic Supercenters, grew from 3 to 344.

Profit margin: This has slipped in recent years, and is holding at 2.9 percent, probably because of a slowed growth in total sales.

Based on this analysis, we would say that Wal-Mart is a good investment that is showing the signs of a maturing company. Although there have been some negative results, the overall picture is of a strong retailer that is slowing in growth but one that is managed well and it still making a decent return for its investors.

Ann Brewer concludes an annual report "is all about management and changes that you don't always get in the *Value Line* summaries. You don't base a decision to sell or to buy on the annual report. But it's a helpful tool."

So have patience with yourself if at first reading annual reports seems difficult. With enough practice, it can be so helpful and fun you'll find yourself eagerly checking your mailbox for that next juicy report to read.

CHAPTER TEN

Knowing When to Sell

Before we describe how to recognize when it is time to sell, we would like to emphasize an important point from one of our previous books, *The Beardstown Ladies' Stitch-in-Time Guide to Growing Your Nest Egg*: Once you begin building a portfolio of stock investments, heed the old adage "Don't put all of your eggs in one basket."

Your basket, of course, is your stock portfolio. As you become more experienced as an investor, you will undoubtedly find some real stock-market winners. You might then be tempted to invest more and more of your available funds in one or two terrific companies (your golden eggs). Just remember to hedge your bets: no matter how good a stock is, it's best not to let it take up more than 10 percent of your entire stock investment portfolio. If that stock grows past 10 percent, you might want to sell some and invest that money in other promising stocks. The key is to protect yourself with a diversity of stock investments. That way, if one stock falls upon hard times, it can only affect 10 percent or less of your portfolio.

Now then, what about selling a stock that does fall on hard times? Ask any ten stock investors to describe when to sell your stock and you will end up with ten different answers. That's understandable, since the decision to sell a stock is based on individual investment goals, personalities, and even certain feelings. It's an art more than a science.

Our investment philosophy is focused on long-term investing: Find a promising stock, thoroughly evaluate it, buy it, and then give it time to gain in value. Ruth explains, "We don't try to time the market. Just because it goes down, we don't sell out. In fact, we think maybe that's the time to buy while the prices are low." We stick with our stocks for the long haul because experience has shown us that a good stock should make money for us if we give it enough time.

The most common mistake people make is selling a stock too soon, according to Ann Corley. "Years ago when my husband was investing in stocks they weren't appreciating like they have in recent years. It's been different. That's one thing I've learned from the club, that you hold for the long term. In well-managed companies, stock prices usually go up."

There have been occasions, however, when giving a stock time to grow does not work. Once we invested in Fur Vault, a retailer of fine fur coats and other products. Unfortunately, a European fur boycott and actions by animal rights extremists put the brakes on fur sales. Fur Vault's stock went into a tailspin, yet we doggedly held. By the time we finally decided to sell, we had lost $853.66, or 72.4 percent.

The point of the Fur Vault experience is that long-term investors sometimes have to reluctantly cut their losses and sell their stock. In another instance that we'd rather forget, we sold our stock in Wendy's after its selling price had steadily dropped. After we sold our stake in Wendy's, analysts recommended it to buy.

The tricky part is knowing when to sell.

In truth, says Betty, knowing when to sell is harder than knowing when to buy. "We watch our investments. We do a new stock selection guide at least once a year on all of our stocks. As long as growth is still predicted, we like to hold. If, for some reason, the growth isn't predicted, we sell. We also sell when a company's earnings trend is going down or simply when we need some money."

If you are having doubts about keeping your money invested in a particular stock, ask yourself two questions: first, is the stock in question performing substantially lower than your expectations? Our club buys stock with the goal of doubling each investment in five years, which works out to about 14.7 percent growth per year. If a stock is getting a much lower rate of growth, we reevaluate keeping that stock in our portfolio.

Our second question addresses the other side of the coin: has our stock been "a flash in the pan," that strongly performed beyond our expectations and then suddenly took a dive? Are future growth prospects for that stock unlikely? If the answer is yes to either or both questions, we believe that the money invested in that particular stock would be more effective in another investment.

There are several other factors that could influence a decision to sell a stock. A management change, for example, especially in a smaller company, can have an enormous impact on stock performance—for better or for worse. Substantial business lost to superior competitors, a company that is dependent on one product for its success, burgeoning debt, and diminishing profit margins are all telltale signs to reevaluate an investment. In the rest of this chapter, we'll look at each potential For Sale sign.

For Sale Sign #1: The stock is performing well below your long-term goals. Almost every stock will occasionally dip in price. The price of that stock could remain suppressed for weeks or even months, and then rebound in a healthy way. If your stock's selling price goes into a dive, don't panic and sell right away. Call the company and/or contact your broker if you are using a full-service firm. Check the stock's ratings in the *Standard & Poor's 500*. Better yet, see what *Value Line* has to stay about it. Try to pin down what is causing the stock price to dip. If the price is being driven down by a marketwide depression of stock prices, don't sell. We believe that periodic drops in overall market prices are times to put money *into* healthy stocks that will rebound as the market collectively noses upward again. Besides, you probably will lose money by selling it in a depressed market.

Here's our point: If your company is healthy, it will continue to grow in value in spite of some rough spots along the way. Sometimes the stock price will dip and sometimes the price will remain stagnant for several weeks. But if you've done your homework, hang on to your stock, the price should go back up.

Let's look at South Dakota computer maker Gateway 2000, for example. In the early spring of 1997, Gateway's stock had taken a plunge due to strong and increasing competition. Over the summer, however, Gateway rebounded, and by September, the stock was nearly double what it was in March.

Why did Gateway recover? It is a well-managed company with good products and a healthy market share. Although Gateway performed below most people's goals that spring, the overall structure of the company remained strong—and a rebound was, in our opinion, inevitable. Gateway stockholders who panicked and sold in June probably had a lot of second thoughts come fall.

On the other hand, if the price continues to slide for months on end and your research shows that the company's fundamentals are weak, with little or no prospect for improvement—well, then it's probably wise to sell, even if it means a loss. Otherwise you risk losing even more. Redirecting your money to a more promising investment, you can greatly increase your chance for further profitability.

For Sale Sign #2: The stock has surpassed your expectations and any future growth is unlikely. Sometimes a stock's growth will lag behind schedule. Other times a stock will shoot up in value, exceeding our investment goals and doubling our money in less than five years. You'd think anyone would be thrilled if that happens, right? Sometimes such growth is good, sometimes it isn't.

Why? Because, like the race between the tortoise and the hare, a fast-growing stock can tire itself out before it goes the distance. A new stock that shoots up in value might be buoyed by media reports that create a buying frenzy that, in turn, drives up the price so the stock becomes overvalued. At this point, you must determine whether your fast-moving stock will quickly burn itself out like the rabbit or if that stock might continue to grow.

When a stock reaches our investment goal— usually doubling in price within five years—we do a complete evaluation of the stock's health and future growth prospects using the same evaluation that we used before we bought it. We conduct this evaluation whether the stock reaches our investment goal after five years or after fifteen months!

After evaluating our stock, we ask ourselves the following questions: Is it still a strong, well-managed company? Are its growth prospects still looking good? If so, we'll keep it. If not, it's time to sell.

We bought W. A. Kruger for $8 a share and within 15 months sold it at $16 when a new stock selection guide didn't show any continued growth. **For Sale Sign #3: Management changes are having a negative effect.** You no doubt realize that a bungling leader can lead a country or a business to ruination. By the same token, many startup companies are held together by the sheer entrepreneurial energy of their founders: when that leader leaves, the company can't survive. For example, some people say Apple Computer fell on hard times when the forward-looking founder Steve Jobs left the company.

If the company behind your stock has a change in command, it is time to take a close look. Go to your library and have the resource librarian help you search for a recent article on that company in *The Wall Street Journal* and in other financial publications such as *Value Line*. If you have a full-service stockbroker handling your business, this is the time for that broker to earn his or her pay: ask the broker's opinion about selling your stock and ask for any articles or analysis on your company and its new management.

We have been fortunate that we haven't had this problem to date.

For Sale Sign #4: Competition is cutting into the company's business. It's easy to be successful when you have a good product with no competitors. But competitors are as inevitable as death and taxes. Even the best companies can be seriously hurt by a direct competitor who is making a better product than theirs, one that is cheaper to buy, or one that is more reliable.

If Brand X is doing a better job than your company and your company is not responding by doing an even better job, it probably is time to stop and rethink your whole investment in the company. Ask yourself (or better yet, ask a good broker) how much the competition affects the growth potential of your stock. Strong competition that cuts into your company isn't necessarily a reason to sell, but it should be a clue to closely monitor that stock.

For Sale Sign #5: Your company's success or failure depends on a single product or kind of service whose glory days are over. The same principles that apply to maintaining a diversified portfolio often apply to how a company does its business. A company whose fortunes ride on a single product may be riding for a tumble. It's hard for a company to remain stable throughout the normal ups and downs of everyday occurrences without a diversified product line or a variety of services. A diversified company with several products can sustain strong competition and losses in one area without being seriously hurt.

One of Maxine's favorite companies may have suffered from being single-minded. She says, "At the time we bought Cooper Tire, new cars were so expensive and people were having to drive their cars longer. So I thought, 'They're going to need a new set of tires. They can't afford Goodyear and so forth.' Cooper Tire was making and selling tires for used cars. I felt they'd at least seem like new tires to the average person, or the not so wealthy person.

"Business was good, but you're not going to buy a new set of tires all the time. The club just sold it last month. It bothered me. But the figures were saying we should sell. So I had to be honest. You get married to a company. I felt like I was getting a divorce."

For a more dramatic example, let's say a hypothetical company called Happy Hog makes nothing but a pork-rind snack. Suppose the Surgeon General comes out with a report that details the high cholesterol in pork-rind snacks: Demand would fall off and the company would be left holding a lot of bags of pork rinds, with no other products to sell that would keep its all-important cash flow going.

For Sale Sign #6: Your stock's profit margins are declining, or the financial structure of the company is deteriorating. Every company exists to make profit, and the more its profit outpaces its expenses, the healthier the company is. The profit margin is a yardstick that measures how far into the "green" a company is.

Profit margins are calculated by dividing profit by sales. A narrow profit margin means that profits are barely ahead of expenses; a wide profit margin, in contrast, indicates a healthier company.

The profit margin of a business can be compared to the balance in your household checkbook. Both profit margin and checkbook balance indicate how close you are to making ends meet or going broke. A profit margin, like a checkbook balance, reflects cash flow. Cash goes into your checkbook in the form of weekly deposits and expenses drain cash out as you write checks, just as revenues and liabilities work against each other in a business.

For the sake of comparison, let's look at the checkbooks of two families, the Smiths and the Browns. The living expenses for both families are almost identical, but the Smiths have a slightly higher household income and they are frugal spenders. As a result, the balance in the Smith's checkbook is $3,200.62. The balance in the Browns' checkbook is $627.50.

Both the Smiths and the Browns have positive balances and both families are more than making ends meet. However, the larger balance that the Smiths maintain puts them in a much stronger financial position.

What if both families want to add a second bathroom? The bathroom for both will cost $3,000 or $4,000 and the loan payments will be $200 per month. It is clear that the Smiths will be in a much better position than the Browns are to afford the $200 monthly loan payments to pay off the addition.

A greater checkbook balance—or profit margin—enables a family or a company to safely invest more money. It also enables the family or company to weather unexpected expenses, such as a broken water heater. That is why profit margin is important to watch: the smaller a company's profit margin, the closer it is to having its "checkbook" go into the red. If a company's profit margin continues to decrease over time, it is time to reevaluate the company. How much time? Some experienced investors are alarmed by declining profit margins within a period of several months; others say to look at a decrease from one annual report to another. We think if a company's earnings have decreased for three consecutive quarters, it's time to start seriously thinking about selling the stock.

Debt, of course is another warning sign. If the Browns take on too many home improvement projects, the additional bills could eat up their checkbook balance and they might have to borrow money to pay their bills. Companies do this too, and when your stock is showing increasing debt, the company may be borrowing money to make ends meet. If this is the case with your stock, consider it a "sell me" sign.

Just remember that selling a stock is a lot like buying a stock. You have to evaluate an investment by the methods we've described in earlier chapters. Are several of the indicators still positive? If so, you probably should hang on to that stock. If you are thinking about selling a stock, review our six For Sale signs. When several indicators confirm a problem with the stock, it is time to sell.

Once you know it's time to sell, it still can be hard to let go of a stock. After all, you liked it enough to buy it in the first place, so chances are you've gotten fairly attached to it—especially if you've held on to it for the long haul, as we tend to do. Within the club, we have to try not to take it too personally when we make a decision to sell.

"It seems like every time I get a company to follow, it gets sold," laments Elsie. "I still follow Quaker Oats. It had been doing so well and then they bought Snapple and the price went down. I have so much history on it that I am partial to it. I hope that we will consider it again."

Maxine feels the same way about "her" company, Cooper Tires. "We may buy it again some time. I do believe in what they're doing. I see their advertisement on TV. I still watch them."

Hope springs eternal in the heart of a Beardstown Lady and her favorite stock.

NAIC's Six Golden Rules for When NOT to Sell

1. Don't sell just because the price hasn't moved. As long as the fundamentals are strong, have patience.

2. Don't sell because of a paper loss. A paper loss or paper profit is a loss or profit that you would make if you sold your stock at a particular price. These gains or losses are nothing more than calculations made on a piece of paper; they do not become real until your stock is actually sold. For example, if you bought 10 shares of a stock at $10 a share and the stock fell to $5, you would have a paper loss of $50. If you held on to the stock another month and the price rose to $6 before you sold it, your actual loss would be $40. So focus on the fundamentals, not a declining market, which may pull the price of strong stocks down in the short run.

3. Don't sell because of a paper profit. If you sell automatically when a stock hits a predetermined price, you risk missing out on even more profit. If the fundamentals and growth

prospects remain strong, don't part with that
stock!

4. Don't sell on temporary bad news. If the
   long-term view looks bright, hold on for the
   ride.

5. Don't sell just to take action. Holding is as
   meaningful an action as buying or selling.

6. Don't sell a stock that has fallen so far that
   your remaining downside risk is small compared to the upside potential. You have no-
   where to go but up.

CHAPTER ELEVEN

How to Use the Internet for Investing

The internet can be a valuable investment tool for the stock buyer. It is an extremely fast and often accurate information source, most of the information is available for free, and it can save you time and money when you trade stocks online.

Before you get acquainted with the internet, it can seem like a mysterious, complicated realm best suited to high-tech hackers and computer engineers. The internet is simply an interconnected, world-wide network of computers that can communicate with each other. The people who search the internet explore websites, (also called web pages) that are much like the pages of a magazine. Some of us have learned that the internet is surprisingly easy to understand and to use. The key is to go slowly and not let yourself feel intimidated.

Although Ann Corley doesn't yet have a computer, she hopes to get one soon, and with the help of her knowledgeable son, learn all about the internet. "I don't think you ever get too old to learn," she says. "But you have to get interested. A lot of elderly ladies wouldn't want to study."

Many, many people have taken the time to explore the online world, however. As of January 1997, one in four Americans aged 18 and older used an online system in their homes, offices, or elsewhere, according to Roper Starch Worldwide, a consumer research firm in New York. If you include the relatively computer-literate generation that is now in its teens, the share of Americans who use the internet probably is much higher.

Shirley can attest to that: she bought computers, not only for her children, but for her grandchildren as well. Shirley says, "My daughter is on the internet and she and her children e-mail back and forth."

If you are more like most of us Ladies—Shirley herself doesn't yet own a computer—and not completely familiar with the internet, we suggest that you check your local library or bookstore and read one of the many excellent books that describe the internet and how to use it.

Then we highly recommend that you give it a try, as we have been learning to do. According to Carol, using the internet for stocks is going to be the coming thing. "For Christmas I hope to get a modem on my computer." Her only concern is, "I know if I get one, I'm going to be sitting at the computer a lot. The housework's going to be let go even more than it is now."

You can obtain accurate information as a stock investor from many of the same reputable sources that you would contact by phone, in person, or through the mail. One of the most significant differences is that you can access information from your home or office, anytime of day or night. Buffy swears by the convenience of the internet, not to buy stocks, but to do research. She explains, "It doesn't give you as much as the regular *Value Line* does. But, *Value Line* is expensive and maybe I don't have time to go to the library. Besides the library in Beardstown closes real early. It's convenient to be able to look up information on a company I'm researching whenever I want."

Some of the familiar "faces" you will find on the internet are *Value Line* and *The Wall Street Journal*, plus brokerage houses such as Charles Schwab & Co., Smith Barney, and A. G. Edwards. You can find web pages for the American Stock Exchange, the New York Stock Exchange, the National Association of Investors Corporation, and many others. Even small, individual brokers maintain their own websites and so do many private individuals.

One very important point to remember about the internet is that, because it's still so new, it is basically unregulated; it is the Wild West of the communications world. Anybody with access to a computer can post a website on the internet. In addition, computer technology is evolving far faster than any regulatory government agency can keep up with. As a result, the information you can find about financial services—or any subject—on the internet ranges from high quality and trustworthy to unreliable and not useful.

Interactive chat rooms and bulletin boards, where internet users can post messages and write back and forth, exist for any topic that you can think of. While they may provide some useful tips and advice, you have absolutely no way of knowing who is behind the contributions. You have no way of knowing whether the relatively anonymous person who is dispensing investment advice is a fiscal genius or, just as likely, a know-it-all who doesn't really know much at all.

So when traveling online you need to read carefully in order to reach a comfortable destination. It's best to use sources you already are familiar with from a non-internet setting. For example, if you come upon the website of a well-known broker, you can be pretty sure of the company's legitimacy. However, if you come upon a website such as the fictitious "Weird Harold's Cut-Rate Stocks and Bonds," you would be wise take some steps to verify the legitimacy and reputation of the company before you do business with it.

Financial Information Resources on the Internet

People use the internet for countless reasons: they use it to shop for cars, they use it to send electronic messages to other lonely hearts, they use it to make vacation reservations, and they even use it to search for Thanksgiving turkey stuffing recipes.

Doris, who is an elementary school principal, says, "We are trying to gain access to the internet in our school. It's a process. We have a computer lab now and all the classes go, one class at a time. So the children can learn how to use the computer. We're already getting a new lab because our computers are rather obsolete."

While children use the internet to learn their three Rs, we use the internet to get answers to our questions about companies that we might invest in. We also use the internet to find quick stock quotes and to get a company's annual report in a matter of minutes instead of waiting days for it to arrive in the mail.

Betty, who says she's "just learning" about the internet, recently logged on CNN Today for some stock prices. "I got on Stock Quotes and was able to print out a couple of news articles. I'm using it for the latest quotes.

"I think the information is wonderful," she continues. "I've wanted to be able to get the very latest trading information for a long time because I deal with brokerage customers and investment clubs at the bank where I work."

Suppose you were interested in buying stock for, say, Campbell's Soup. You could talk about it with your stockbroker or with other smart investors you know—and we think you should. But you can also do some quick homework on Campbell's Soup (or any company) from your own computer via the internet. Here's how:

The first step is finding the familiar Campbell's Soup logo among the millions of websites out there. It's easy to do; just use a computer program called a search engine. Search engines are designed to find specific information on the internet. Many search engines are available for free and they often are just a click away in popular browsers such as Netscape Navigator or Internet Explorer. (If you are unfamiliar with browser software, once again we suggest going to the library or bookstore for a how-to book about the internet.)

Conducting an internet search actually is easier than using the Yellow Pages (which are also on the internet). All you have to do is type in Campbell's Soup and click the search button. In a matter of seconds, several results will pop up; among them will be the Campbell's Soup home page website address, www.campellsoup.com.

Just click on that address or type it into your browser—and you are there. You'll find the Campbell's Soup website, like most corporate home pages, is colorful and interesting. There is a *Site Map* that operates like an automatic tour guide; just click on it and it will give out directions for getting around the site. You can find information ranging from the company's annual report to a recipe for baked ramen. There is a link to a page that describes new products from Campbell's, information about the many countries in which the company's products are sold, and a link to a page on the company's 125-year history. The page also includes a link that enables you to provide feedback to the company or to submit questions. This handy question-and-answer feature is present on virtually all corporate websites.

All of that is fine and dandy, but you are interested in Campbell's Soup as an investment. If you look at the bottom of the page, you find the *Financial* category. Clicking on it takes you to the Campbell's *Financial Center* web page.

Looking down the page, you find a highlighted link that you can click on to read the Annual Report. You have the option of reading it online or downloading, which means electronically transferring it directly to your computer where you can save it for future reference. You also have the option of printing the report out on your desktop printer.

The online version of an annual report offers much of the same entertaining graphics that the printed version does. But the important point is that the online version contains the same investor information that the printed version contains, including Campbell's annual sales, price per share, profit margin, and others—all at your fingertips—and it's available right now.

Campbell's annual report includes features such

as its *Financial Highlights*, which provides a quick overview of the company's fiscal performance. It includes Campbell's net sales and the company stock dividends and price per share. It also notes the percent change of these stock evaluation measures, for example that Campbell's stock shot up by 43 percent in 1996.

As you flip back and forth between the financial page and the many links it contains, you'll also discover that Campbell's has been making condensed soup since 1897; that its product line includes Godiva chocolate, Pepperidge Farm baked goods, and Pace Mexican salsa; and that Campbell's recently bought Erasco, the leading soup company in Germany.

Beyond the Corporate Web

A host of other sites where you can get answers to your questions about investments, are even more objective and therefore more useful. Like a fee-based financial planner site with nothing to sell you other than its service is bound to provide a more complete picture of a company.

Financial Web (www.financialweb.com), for example, lists stock quotes, annual reports, and other stock-investor information. CNN maintains a financial news page (www.cnnfn.com) where you can scan the latest business news. *Value Line* provides its useful information to web surfers at its website as well (www.valueline.com).

It's worth spending some time to "surf" the internet to discover other useful, third-party sites that don't appear to be sponsored by any specific for-profit firms to answer your questions or provide important investor news. (See page 279 for a list.)

Stock Trading and Banking on the Internet

The popularity of internet stock trading and banking is growing because of its inherent speed, lower cost, and convenience. When you trade online, banker's hours are whatever hours you choose. You can post an order to buy stock at 2 A.M. or 2 P.M., any day of the week. Of course, the trade cannot be made until the stock exchange opens, but you can place an order whenever you choose.

Many stock brokers encourage their clients to use the internet for trading because it saves them a lot of time and money. As a result, brokers pass the savings on to you. For example, one leading discount broker offers a 20 percent discount below its normal commissions for transactions that are made electronically rather than in person or by phone. (See chart on broker's fees in Chapter Eight on page 211.)

You can use the same method for choosing an online broker on the internet as you do for choosing a broker off-line. We recommend that you use the methods that we described in Chapter Eight for choosing your stockbroker—just add another question about whether that broker uses a "secure" site for trading. (See section on internet security below.)

Well-designed stockbrokers' web pages will have built-in security features and an easy-to-follow menu that take you through the steps of stock trading on the internet. We will show you how to begin online trading by using one broker, Charles Schwab & Co, as an example. Schwab's website address is: www.schwab.com/SchwabNOW.

One feature that we particularly like on Schwab's site (and some others) is a set of demonstrations that take you through simulated stock purchases, sales, and other financial transactions. These simulated transactions allow you to learn how to buy and sell stocks online without committing any money. On Schwab's site, one demonstration takes you, step by step, through the purchase of 100 shares of IBM stock.

On Schwab's web page, there is a list of options and some important information—including a notice that the demonstrations all are simulated transactions only. The demonstration options include obtaining stock quotes, checking on orders placed, checking account balances, and contacting the broker by electronic e-mail.

On the right side of the Schwab web page, click on the highlighted word demo, where the page urges you to "Try Web Trading Now." One click of your computer mouse will take you to Schwab's demonstration page, where you can try simulated stock buys, sells, or you can check stock quotes, account balances, the status of your order, and several other features. Follow the instructions for conducting a simulated trade. There will be several choices you can make, such as buying mutual funds and other investments. For our purposes, let's choose a stock buy of 100 shares of IBM at market price. Your computer will take you to an online order blank where you follow the instructions and fill in your simulated purchase of 100 shares of IBM stock.

Once you've filled in the online order blank, you'll click the "submit" button. Your order is then displayed and you are asked to verify it. The display notes that you are buying 100 shares of IBM at the current market price of $92, with an estimated purchase price of $9,317.45. The commission is $40. If you agree, click the "place order" button on the screen. An order verification appears noting your order number and telling you that your order has been received. That's all there is to it!

Of course, you must establish an account with your online broker before you conduct an actual stock transaction. The instructions for doing that are included on the broker's web page. Many people choose to call their online brokers on the phone to set up their accounts before trading online. Once you've set up your account, you simply log onto the broker's website and enter a PIN number just like the one you use at your bank's ATM.

After your PIN is accepted, you can check your account balance, or click on a button that will take you to an online order form to buy stock. You fill in the blanks, click on a button and your order is instantly submitted.

Once you are familiar with the web, shop around: if you look hard enough, you will find a wide array of online stock traders that offer a variety of services at a variety of prices. Discount and deep discount traders are most numerous. For example, Datek Securities Corp. (www.datek.com) has advertised a commission of $9.99 per trade.

The beauty of good internet broker sites is that they take you through a trade in an easy, step-by-step process—and you don't have to get dressed up or even leave home to conduct your investment business. It's also statistically probably as safe, if not safer, to trade online than to use any other method. In the following section, we'll explain what we mean by that.

Internet Security

It goes without saying that you should be careful not to reveal information about yourself while you are using the internet. However, there are protections for people who buy and sell stocks and do their banking on the internet. That security is provided by "secure" websites, which have hacker-resistant protections built into them. This allows people to use account numbers and credit card numbers on the internet with little fear of hacker, or unauthorized electronic thief, reading that information.

These secure sites bill themselves as being safe for the investor and actually, they are safer than many of your normal non-internet activities, such as using a credit card. Think about it: almost daily, you provide your credit card number to waiters, gas station attendants, supermarket cashiers, and anonymous clerks in mail-order catalogs. Yet there is a perception that internet shopping is somehow less safe.

Stockbrokers who trade online typically have built-in security systems that enable their customers to buy and sell stocks safely. For example, discount broker Charles Schwab & Co. puts all of its critical information into a coded website through a process that is called encryption. Account numbers, passwords, and stock orders are also encrypted.

One way that you can determine if you are logged on to a secure web site is to simply look at your computer screen: If you have an advanced internet browser software such as Internet Explorer or Netscape Navigator, or America Online's browser, a little symbol called an icon will appear when you are logged onto a secure site. The secure site icons are different for each browser. For example, Netscape Navigator uses an icon of a key to alert the user that he or she is on a secure site while Microsoft's Internet Explorer uses a padlock icon.

If you're still worried, there is the option of using the Internet for investor research and then getting off your computer and making your trade the old-fashioned ways: in person or over the phone. This option capitalizes on the internet's speed and accessibility while eliminating the worry of a computer hacker reading sensitive information such as your account number.

Some of Our Favorite Websites

We really enjoy using the internet to monitor our investments. It is convenient to sit down with your morning coffee and log onto your broker's website to check your investments, keep track of your portfolio, or to leisurely read that day's financial news on *The Wall Street Journal* website. Here are some of the websites that we find interesting or useful. Try these and explore some of your own.

- AMEX: The American Stock Exchange. Address: www.amex.com. This neat homepage lists leading indexes such as the Dow, Standard & Poor's, and, of course, the AMEX. It also lists most active stocks on that exchange.
- *Annual Reports Online*. Address: www.annualre portsonline.com. This site provides free and easy access to many annual reports.
- *CNNfn*: The CNN Financial Network page. Ad-

dress: www.cnnfn.com. A quick look at the news from a business point of view. Interesting, colorful, and easy to use.

- *DRIP Investor.* All about dividend reinvestment plans and no-load stocks. Address: www.dripin vestor.com.
- *Financial Web.* Provides links to several online financial publications, such as *The Wall Street Journal*, plus many answers and ideas for the online investor. Address: www.financialweb.com.
- *Hoover's Online.* If you want to search company profiles or see a complete list of company websites, this is the place. Address: www.hoovers. com.
- *NAIC Online.* The home page of the National Association of Investors Corporation. Address: www.better-investing.org. Every thing you ever wanted to know about the NAIC, including how to join and how to invest through this not-for-profit organization.
- *NASDAQ* home page. The home page of the over-the-counter National Association of Securities Dealers Automated Quotation System. Address: www.nasdaq.com. Check major indices, get market news, and more.
- *NYSE* home page. The online headquarters of the New York Stock Exchange. Address: www. nyse.com. Find listed companies, market information, and more.
- *The Online Investor* home page. Address: www.

investhelp.com. This home page is packed with information, advice and answers to your questions about investing online.

- *Pointcast Network.* This free service lets you program it to scan for news and other information that it automatically brings back to your computer. You can monitor stock quotes, check sports scores, or read the *Los Angeles Times* at your leisure. Address: www.pointcast.com.

- *U.S. Securities and Exchange Commission.* The federal regulator of the stock market has its own home page too. Address: www.sec.gov/index.html. If you want to know the rules or file a complaint, here is a good place to start. A complete listing of U.S. government agency websites can be found on the *U.S. Federal Government Agencies Page.* Address: www.lib.lsu.edu/gov/fedgov.

- *Value Line* home page. Yes, one of our favorite investment advice and information sources is online. Address: www.valueline.com. Why go to the library to read *Value Line* when you can get a lot of the information right at home on your computer!

- *The Wall Street Journal Interactive Edition.* Read many of the articles in our favorite financial newspaper online. Address: www.wsj.com.

- *Web Investors' Dictionary.* Address: www.webinvestors.com. Just like the title says, an alphabetically ordered source of definitions to investing and online investing terms and concepts.

CHAPTER TWELVE

Ask the Ladies

No matter how many books we write, wherever we go people still have questions for us. In fact, sometimes it seems the more we write, the more questions we're asked! We think that's great: it means people are thinking about things and want to know even more. We also believe there is never a stupid question.

In this chapter, we've collected some of the questions we're asked most frequently as we travel around the country for workshops, book signings, and other appearances. Although you may find the information in other parts of this book, this is the only place we provide a question and answer format, which many people seem to appreciate.

How do you find the companies that you invest in?

We use *Value Line*'s screening system, "Timely Stocks in Timely Industries." We like to invest in companies whose products or services we use. We watch the buying trends.—*Betty Sinnock*

Do you have a favorite stock?

Yes, RPM. We bought it back in 1984 for 5.99—one of our first stocks. I bought it for myself and am very pleased.—*Ruth Huston*

My favorite stock is Wolverine World Wide. I know the Wolverine boot is durable and I like the Hush Puppy shoes. This stock has done very well for the club. I was one of the Ladies who attended the annual meeting a few years ago. The officers treated us royally. Also Wolverine let each of the Beardstown Ladies order a pair of shoes free from their spring catalog which was nice. You know we Ladies like shoes, and free ones to boot!—*Ann Brewer*

I do have a favorite stock. It is Intel, a technology stock, which I have owned since 1993 and in which I have a nice profit. Intel supplies the computing industry with the pentium chips, boards, systems, and software for computers. It is an exciting stock (volatile) as there are always new things happening with Intel, such as a faster chip. There is usually an article on Intel in *The Wall Street Journal* every day.—*Ann Corley*

People want to know if I have a hot tip for them. I don't have a hot tip.—*Shirley Gross*

Quaker Oats was a great stock to follow. There is so much history, all very interesting. I still follow

the price even though we sold it. I'm hesitant to buy it on my own, but I may in the future.
—*Elsie Scheer*

Do you use the Stock Selection Guide every time you study a new company?

Yes!—*The Beardstown Ladies*

How should my portfolio be allocated?

Each person's portfolio is different due to age and needs. A younger investor may want to have more money in stocks than an older person. They have a longer time to recover should the market take a downturn. One should have bonds, stocks, and "safe" investments.—*Ann Brewer*

A portfolio allocation is important to your investment success, and you need to know what percentage of your assets are in the three broad categories of stocks (growth), bonds (fixed income), and cash (CDs, short term, depending on interest rates, savings accounts, and money market funds). You may have to rebalance from time to time.—*Ann Corley*

Diversify. Do not buy in all one industry like medical companies or electronic companies or food companies.—*Ruth Huston*

Allocate your portfolio according to your financial worth and how much risk you personally want to take.—*Elsie Scheer*

What do you mean when you say diversify?

We mean that we try to invest in different-sized companies and in different industries. We like to have different-size companies: 25 percent small capitalization, 50 percent mid-capitalization, and 25 percent large blue chip companies.—*Betty Sinnock*

What should I invest in?

We can't answer that question. We encourage you to study, use your own judgment, and make your own decisions.—*Betty Sinnock*

It varies so much with where you are in the whole program. Our biggest audience have been people who suddenly realize, oh, I probably could do this. I tell them that what we're going to give them is pretty elementary because we're not licensed as advisers. It has to be their decision—that's what it's all about. We're telling you that you can play a part in your future and in your investment plan.—*Carnell Korsmeyer*

Contribute as much as you can to a 401K (pretax dollars, employer contributes also), Keogh (self-employment, tax deferred), and IRA (tax-deferred plan and other retirement savings). Stocks are another choice. Over the long term, stocks have outperformed other investments, and the general direction of the stock market has been up. Another choice might be bonds or mutual funds, or both. However, you need to understand what you are investing in, whether it be stocks, bonds, or mutual funds.—*Ann Corley*

Yourself. Have a plan that you feel comfortable with and stick with it. Nothing is worse than being a worrier and not being able to sleep at night.
—*Ann Brewer*

Invest in growth stocks and industries you know something about through your research. Do your homework.—*Ruth Huston*

We are not supposed to recommend any specific stocks, because if people invest and lose money, then they can come back and say, "You told me it was good" and we can get sued. So we have to be very careful. We can't say we recommend this, we can only tell them the stocks we have in our club.—*Sylvia Gaushell*

A lot of people say give us some tips on stocks to look at. We don't want them to think we're rude because we don't give tips, but we're not licensed with SEC, so that is why we cannot give tips. We jokingly say, "Our best tip is buy our book."
—*Buffy Tillitt-Pratt*

I try to tell people don't go out and buy a stock because we've got it. It was in the buy range when we bought it, but it might not be now. We don't want people to be buying it at the wrong time.
—*Ruth Huston*

How can I invest without risk?

Any investment involves some degree of risk, and one of the most important factors to consider in choosing your investments is your ability to handle risk. The higher the return, the more risk. Stocks are risky in the short term, so buy for the long term and buy growth stocks. One way to balance risk and reward is to diversify—spread your money among a variety of investments.—*Ann Corley*

Don't do anything you would let worry you or keep you awake at night.—*Elsie Scheer*

Don't put all your eggs in one basket. Diversify.—*Ruth Huston*

How much time does it take to learn about the stock market and to invest?

A lot of people are worried about how much time it takes. But look at how people are hooked on the internet and how much time they spend on the internet. If you're going to spend time on the internet, look at some stocks.—*Carol McCombs*

You can't explain what the stock market is in fifteen or twenty minutes. The most concise way I can put it is that you're buying a little portion of a company when you invest in it.—*Buffy Tillitt-Pratt*

I have had phone calls from people who say tell me all about the stock market. They want to know how to evaluate the stock market and how to buy stocks in a ten-minute telephone conversation. It cannot be done. It takes time and learning.
—*Shirley Gross*

How do I find money to invest?

Keep asking yourself, "Do I want it or need it?" Learn what the word "save" is.—*Elsie Scheer*

It's not how much money you make, but what you do with it after you make it. Pay yourself first. Your nest egg will grow a lot faster if you spend less and save more. In *The Beardstown Ladies' Guide to Smart Spending for Big Savings* we say, "Think about what you are spending money on before you buy anything. Avoid emotional spending and buy only what you need. Remember, once you spend that money, it's gone."—*Ann Corley*

Check your finances to see what you really need. When purchasing an item, check out several and see what fits your budget best.—*Ruth Huston*

Can I give you money to invest for me?

No, we are not licensed or registered. We just want to share what we have learned to help you get started.—*Betty Sinnock*

How can I get started?

We like for you to buy our books. We also recommend that you join the National Association of Investors Corporation for the education information that is in *Better Investing*, their monthly magazine.—*Betty Sinnock*

Do you see a bull or bear market in the future?

I guess the answer is yes.—*Carnell Korsmeyer*

Nobody can forecast the market's direction. —*Ann Corley*

We don't try to time the market.—*Ruth Huston*

What's the weather going to be in the future? Who really knows?—*Elsie Scheer*

If we had a crystal ball, we would be millionaires! I believe we will have corrections from time to time. Overall I believe it will stay bullish for the next few years, but then I am no expert.
—*Ann Brewer*

What investment or financial magazines should I read?

Kiplinger's, Money magazine, Forbes. I have *The Wall Street Journal*. I have both *Value Line* regular edition and the expanded edition which is another 1,800 stocks. I have *Morningstar* which follows all the mutual funds. NAIC has also developed a tool where you can compare mutual funds as long as you're comparing the same type of mutual funds to determine which ones you might want to get. I get Standard & Poor's Outlook. They rate their stocks by five stars rather than one to five, with the five stars being the best.—*Betty Sinnock*

Oh, I love *Kiplinger's*. I got started on that at the bank when I worked there. They took it and it seemed like it always ended up on my desk by the time I had gotten to be assistant cashier. So, now I take it. Also, *U.S. News* and *Bottom Line*.
—*Maxine Thomas*

The Wall Street Journal, Investor's Business Daily, Better Investing, BusinessWeek, and *Forbes*.
—*Ann Corley*

The Wall Street Journal. You get a lot of informa-

tion out of that. It tells you if there's any future litigations which you might not read in an annual report. On a day-to-day basis, you can keep up with monitoring your company best through publications like *The Wall Street Journal.*
—*Margaret Houchins*

Kiplinger's, Money, and Fortune.—*Elsie Scheer*

What do you think of the internet as an investment tool?

I have used the internet to do research, not to buy stocks. It doesn't give you what *Value Line* does. But when I don't have time to go to the library, I just punch it up on the internet and I print off the phone number to call for the stockholder relations kit. Or if I want something right now and I don't have time to go to the library, I use the internet. The library in Beardstown closes real early too.
—*Buffy Tillitt-Pratt*

I am not familiar with the internet as I do not have a computer nor access to one. I plan to buy one in the near future and I will check it out.
—*Ann Corley*

You still need to study, study, study before you buy.—*Elsie Scheer*

Do I have to use a broker?

No. But it's just a quicker, common-sense way to go.—*Elsie Scheer*

It depends on how comfortable you are in mak-

ing your own decisions. You don't have to use a full service broker. Today there are discount brokers, on-line brokers, dividend reinvestment plans, and direct purchases through many companies.
—*Betty Sinnock*

No, you can invest through NAIC as an individual.—*Ruth Huston*

No, you do not have to use a broker to buy stocks. There is a dividend reinvestment plan offered by some corporations which allows you to purchase shares of stock directly from them without using a broker.—*Ann Corley*

What do you think about discount brokerages?

If you need advice or information on what stocks to buy or sell, then you should probably have a full service broker, as a discount broker does not give this service. If you do not need any advice and want to make your own decisions on the stocks you plan to buy or sell, then you might want to go with a discount broker. It should be less expensive.
—*Ann Corley*

What is the difference between a stock and a mutual fund?

A stock represents ownership in a company. A mutual fund is an investment vehicle where people buy shares in the mutual fund and a manager invests the money. There are mutual funds in all kinds of investments such as stock, corporate

bonds, municipal bonds, U.S. Treasuries, mix of stocks and bonds, money markets, etc.
—*Betty Sinnock*

A mutual fund investor shares in the profits and losses and income and expense. At the end of the year the investor receives a 1099 showing the dividends and capital gains on their investment for their income tax return. There are closed-end and open-end funds. Open-end funds are divided into load and no-load funds.—*Ann Corley*

What do you think about investing in mutual funds versus individual stocks?

Once you have some investment knowledge, you have a tendency not to put all your eggs in one basket. A little bit of both offers experience and comparison.—*Elsie Scheer*

I think it is a good idea to invest in both mutual funds and individual stocks. Some advantages for buying and holding mutual funds are professional management and division of risk because your dollars are spread over many company stocks and dividends are automatically added for additional shares.—*Ann Corley*

Anyone who does not have time or does not want to take the time to study investments might do well to have one or more mutual funds.—*Betty Sinnock*

How should I go about finding good mutual funds?

A potential investor in mutual funds should read, read, read. *Morningstar* is a publication that does for mutual funds what *Value Line* does for individual stocks. Also, inquire about the fund manager. Are others comfortable with the manager? How has the fund performed?—*Ann Brewer*

I have mutual funds through my bank.—*Ruth Huston*

You would want to send for a prospectus and shareholder report from several mutual funds and then compare them to see which ones you might want to invest in.—*Ann Corley*

Look at different companies' records.—*Elsie Scheer*

When should I sell a stock?

That is more difficult than deciding to buy. We watch our investments and do a new Stock Selection Guide every year on each one. As long as growth is still predicted, we like to hold. If, for any reason, the growth isn't predicted, we sell. We also sell when we see a company trending down in earnings or when we need some money.—*Betty Sinnock*

We don't set a certain dollar figure for when to sell a stock. We watch the stock and keep it for the long term as long as the management is good and it is still showing growth. I know of some individuals who set a certain goal and after the stock reaches that number, they sell.—*Ann Brewer*

Do you have a set amount that you'll pay for a stock?

I don't think you can have a set amount you will pay for a certain stock. It depends upon the company. Our club uses the stock selection guide to help us determine what price to pay. You give more for one stock than you would for another.
—*Ann Corley*

What is the difference between a growth stock and an income stock?

The income stock pays a fairly high dividend which many people need and want. The growth company appreciates in price, so we don't realize a profit until we sell the stock.—*Betty Sinnock*

What is a cyclical stock?

This is a stock that usually has periods of good performance and periods of poor performance. Many stocks tend to have a five-year cycle.—*Betty Sinnock*

What is more important, the P/E ratio or the upside/downside ratio?

We think that they are both very important. We stress that if a current P/E ratio is more than the five-year average, the price is probably too high and if our upside/down ratio isn't at least 3 to 1 we usually look for another company.—*Betty Sinnock*

Glossary

accounts payable: Money owed by a company.

accounts receivable: Money owed to a company for the sale of goods or services.

accrued expense: An expense that has not been paid yet.

accumulated depreciation: The total loss of value of an asset since it was bought.

acid test ratio: The value of a company's marketable securities, cash, and accounts receivable divided by its total current liabilities. Determines whether a company can raise enough cash quickly to cover its debts. A ratio of at least 1:1 is a standard benchmark. Also known as the quick ratio.

aggressive growth stock: Stock that gives the investor the chance to earn above-average returns with above-average risk, usually in a company that is small but expanding rapidly.

American Depository Receipt (ADR): Shares of foreign companies sold in U.S. markets.

American Stock Exchange (AMEX): The second largest U.S. stock exchange.

AMEX Market Value Index: A measurement of the stocks on the American Stock Exchange.

analyst: An individual, usually employed by a brokerage firm, who studies the market and rates stocks and industries.

annual meeting of shareholders: A gathering once a year of owners of stock in a corporation to elect officers, vote on issues, and discuss the company's financial state.

annual report: Yearly publication of a corporation's business covering the past fiscal year, including comprehensive financial statements. Mailed to shareholders; available to the public on request.

appreciation: The increase in value of an asset.

asking price: The price an investor pays for stock.

asset: Something of value to a company or individual. Company assets include machinery, plants, and accounts receivable. Individual assets include homes, savings accounts, securities, collectibles, and insurance policies.

average: A set of calculations that measures the value of sectors of the stock market and the stock market as a whole. Example: Dow Jones Industrial Average.

averaging down: A strategy used by investors to buy additional stock at a lower price than the original purchase price to reduce their average cost per share in anticipation that the stock price will increase.

balance sheet: A financial statement that gives a snapshot of a company's assets, liabilities, and capital on a specific date.

bankruptcy: A condition whereby companies or people declare that they are unable to pay debts.

bear market: An extended period of falling stock prices. Opposite of a bull market.

beta: A number that compares the volatility (movement) of a stock's price relative to that of the total market. A beta of 1 means that a stock price moves up and down at the same rate as the market as a whole. A beta of 2 means that when the market drops or rises 10 percent, the stock price is likely to move double that, or 20 percent. A beta of .5 means that if the market rises 10 percent, the stock will likely rise only 5 percent.

bid price: The price an investor receives for the sale of stock.

blue-chip stock: The stock of a large, stable company, named after the blue chips used in poker games, the chips with the highest value.

board of directors: The group that manages the operation of a corporation.

book value per share: Net worth divided by the number of shares outstanding. This number tells you what each share would be worth if the company was suddenly liquidated, based on balance sheet figures.

broker: An individual who arranges for a transfer in the ownership of security between a buyer and seller. Brokers charge a fee for this service.

bull market: An extended period of rising stock prices. Opposite of a bear market.

business sales and inventories index: Measurement of manufacturing, retail, and wholesale trade sales plus the amount of goods held in inventory not yet sold.

Buttonwood Agreement: The contract signed by twenty-four brokers in 1792 that marked the start of the New York Stock Exchange.

buy-and-hold: An investment strategy that dictates purchasing securities and holding on to them regardless of market fluctuation, relying on the long-term health of the underlying companies.

capital gain: The profit from the sale of a capital asset, such as securities or a home.

capital gains tax: Tax levied on the difference between the cost of a capital asset and the sale price.

capital loss: The loss incurred when a capital asset is sold for less than the price for which it was purchased.

cash flow: The net income of a company plus any noncash deductions from income, such as depreciation. A measure of a company's ability to cover expenses and pay dividends.

cash flow statement: A report of a company's cash flow over a period of time, which gives a good indication of the firm's ability to pay debt.

certificates of deposits (CDs): A bank-issued investment that pays a specified amount of interest depending on the amount of money deposited and the length of time it is kept in the bank, usually from three months to five years.

chart: A graph that shows a stock's price and volume of trading over a period of time.

churning: An illegal practice by a stockbroker whereby the broker advises a client to sell stock soon after it was purchased for no apparent reason other than to earn the broker a commission.

closing price: The price of a stock at the end of a trading session.

commission: The fee charged by a stockbroker or financial adviser in return for services.

common stock: A share of stock that represents a fractional ownership of a corporation and that entitles the holder to have voting rights in the corporation. If the company goes out of business, owners of common stock have last claim on assets after bondholders, other creditors, and preferred stockholders.

convert to cash: Liquidate bonds, CDs, and stocks.

corporation: A business structure created by law and registered with the state. Its shareholders have limited liability.

correction: An overall drop in an overinflated stock market that brings the prices down to more realistic levels.

crash: A sudden large drop in the overall value of stock prices.

credit line: A revolving credit arrangement whereby a borrower has access to a maximum amount over a set period of time.

currency risk: An investment risk caused by fluctuations in currency values.

current assets: Assets that may be converted into cash within a year. They are listed on the balance sheet in the order of the ease with which they can be converted to cash: cash; government securities; accounts receivable; and inventories.

current liabilities: Debts that are due within a year.

current ratio: Current assets divided by current liabilities.

day trader: An investor who buys and sells securities based on short-term price fluctuations.

deep discount broker: A broker who facilitates trades for a reduced commission, but who offers little or no other services.

deflation: A rate at which the prices of goods and services declines in the economy as a whole.

depreciation: An asset's loss of value of a period of time. Stockholders are allowed tax deductions based on depreciation.

derivative: A type of security the value of which is based on another security. Examples are options and futures.

digest of earnings report: A financial document that includes information about a company's quarterly revenues, net income, number of shares outstanding, and earnings per share.

dilution: The decrease in a stock's value caused by an increase in the number of shares outstanding.

disclosure statement: A document a company is required to submit to the Securities and Exchange Commission (SEC) at the time of an initial public offering (IPO) that includes financial information, background of the company's officers, and details about how the company plans to spend the money raised from the sale of stock.

discount broker: A broker who arranges for the transfer of stock ownership for a reduced commission, but who does not offer services or information to clients.

diversify: To spread risk by investing a wide variety of stocks, industries, and/or types of securities.

dividend: A payment issued by a company to stockholders, either in cash or stock, that distributes a portion of its earnings and profits.

Dividend Reinvestment Program (DRIP): An investment system offered by many companies in which dividends may be reinvested for fractional shares of stock.

dividend stock: A stock that pays out regular dividends.

dividend yield: The amount an investment is expected to return to investors calculated by dividing the annual dividend by the current price of the stock.

dollar-cost averaging: An investment strategy whereby one contributes a constant amount to a security at regular intervals, regardless of fluctuations in market price.

Dow Jones Industrial Average (DJIA): The average price of 30 leading U.S. industrial stocks.

Dow Jones Transportation Average: Measurement of the stock prices of 20 railroads, airlines, and trucking companies used to gauge the overall health of the transportation sector of the U.S. economy.

Dow Jones Utility Average: Measurement of the stock prices of 15 gas, oil, electric, and other energy companies.

earnings: A company's net income.

earnings per share (EPS): A figure on an income statement that measures a company's profitability. EPS is calculated by dividing net income by shares outstanding.

earnings predictability: A rating that appears in *The Value Line Investment Survey* that measures the degree to which a company's earnings are predictable based on past performance. Scale: 100 (most predictable) to 5 (least predictable.) No mentionable figure is listed as NMF.

economic risk: An investment risk based on the overall health of the economy. The danger is that if the economy as a whole declines, the value of the investor's portfolio will decline too.

equity: Common and preferred stock.

exchange rate: The value of one currency in relation to the value of a different currency.

expansion: A period of economic growth.

expense ratio: An indication of the health of a company calculated by dividing the expenses by the revenues as they appear on the income statement.

Federal Reserve System: The independent bank that regulates the U.S. money supply.

Federal Trade Commission (FTC): The U.S. government agency that regulates markets by preventing the formation of monopolies and encouraging free trade.

financial adviser: An individual who provides advice on how to identify financial goals and strategies for investing.

financial strength: A rating that appears in *The Value Line Investment Survey* that measures a company's financial condition. Scale: A+ + (strongest) to C (weakest).

fixed assets: Assets, such as property, plant, and equipment, that the company does not expect to convert into cash within a year.

fraud: Making false statements or acting deceptively for personal gain.

full-service broker: A stockbroker who provides services and information to clients in addition to arranging for the transfer of ownership of stock.

fundamental analysis: An investment strategy that evaluates a stock based on a company's growth and profits over a period of time.

fundamentals: The overall financial situation of a company.

going public: Offering stock for sale to the public for the first time.

Great Depression: A period of economic decline during the 1930s that was initiated by the stock market crash of 1929.

growth stock: A stock whose value is expected to increase due to the expansion of its company, revenues, and earnings.

income statement: A document included as part of an annual report that describes a company's profitability over time.

income stock: A stock that pays regular relatively high dividends but is not expected to increase significantly in value.

incorporate: To register a company with the state in which it is located to create an independent entity that separates the firm's liabilities from that of its owners.

index: A measurement of the stock market's performance.

industry rank: A company's rating within its industry based on its timeliness ranking by *The Value Line Investment Survey*.

inflation: The rate at which overall prices rise in the economy.

initial public offering (IPO): The first time stock is offered for sale to the public.

insider trading: An illegal use of information that has not been publicized or disseminated by the company by employees and officers of a company that results in profiting from the manipulation of the stock market and financial gain to those who engaged in the activity.

intangible asset: An asset with no physical properties. An example is goodwill.

inventory: Raw materials and finished goods a company intends to sell.

investment banker: An individual who purchases stock from corporations and offers the stock for sale to investors. Also known as an underwriter.

investment objective: An investor's financial need determines your goal.

large-capitalization stock: The stock of a big company.

liabilities: The claims of creditors.

liquidate: To convert assets to cash.

liquidity: The ability of an asset to be converted to cash.

long-term debt: Debt, such as bonds, secured by company property.

majority shareholder: A shareholder who owns over 50 percent of a company's stock.

margin account: A brokerage account that allows for the purchase of stock on credit based on the value of the client's equity in a securities account. You can use the credit to purchase whatever you want.

margin call: A broker's demand that a client deposit cash in his account to compensate for a decrease in the value of the stocks in the account.

market capitalization: The total value of a company's outstanding shares calculated by multiplying the total number of shares outstanding by the price per share.

market risk: An investment risk based on the potential for the entire stock market to fall.

market timing: An investment strategy that relies on one's ability to predict increases or decreases in the value of particular stocks.

mid-cap stock: The stock of a medium-sized company.

Nasdaq (National Association of Securities Dealers Automated Quotation System): An electronic, screen-based equity market operated and regulated by the National Association of Securities Dealers (NASD).

Nasdaq Composite Index: A measurement of the stock prices of the over-the-counter stocks listed on the Nasdaq system.

National Association of Investors Corporation (NAIC): A nonprofit organization that provides educational materials and programs to individual investors and investment clubs.

National Association of Securities Dealers (NASD): The organization that regulates Nasdaq brokers and dealers and the OTC market.

net income: Profit after taxes.

net sales: The amount of money collected for goods and services sold minus returns and allowances.

net worth: All assets minus all liabilities.

newsgroup: An electronic bulletin board on the internet that allows participants to interact by posting messages and responding to messages posted.

New York Stock Exchange (NYSE): The largest and most active stock market in the world.

NYSE Composite Index: A measurement of all the common stocks listed on the NYSE.

odd lot: Less than 100 shares of stock purchased or sold at one time.

operating costs and expenses: Expenses including the cost of goods sold, marketing, administration, and research and development.

optional dividend: A dividend that can be taken in cash or shares of stock.

over-the-counter (OTC): Describing stocks of generally newer, less established companies that are traded electronically, by telephone, or direct negotiation rather than at a physical stock exchange.

paper loss/paper profit: A loss or profit that you would make if you sold your stock at a particular price, so called because these losses and gains are nothing more than calculations made on a piece of paper. They do not become "real" until the security is actually sold.

peak: The strongest point in an economic cycle.

penny stock: A stock that sells for under $1.

pink sheets: Information about the price of OTC stocks. Typically, these are stocks that do not meet Nasdaq requirements—the smallest, most speculative issues.

portfolio: A group of investments held by an individual investor, institutional investor, or investment club.

preferred stock: A type of stock that guarantees holders fixed dividends but no voting rights. If the company goes out of business, the claims of preferred stockholders to the remains take precedence over common stockholders.

price growth persistence: A rating that appears in *The Value Line Investment Survey* that measures a stock's price performance compared to predictions based on past performance. Scale: 100 (most persistent) to 5 (least).

price-to-book ratio: A measure of a company's value calculated by dividing the share price by the book value per share.

price-to-earnings (PE) ratio: The price of a share of stock divided by the company's earnings per share.

prime rate: A benchmark to which other rates are pegged.

principal amount: The original amount of money invested.

private corporation: A corporation that does not offer stock for sale to the public.

private placement: The sale of stock to private investors not offered to the general public.

profit: Income less expenses.

profit and loss (P&L statement): See income statement.

profit margin: A figure on an income statement calculated by dividing the net income by the revenue.

prospectus: An abbreviated version of the disclosure statement required by the SEC. A prospectus is used to sell stock during an initial public offering (IPO) and includes financial information about the company, a business plan, background of the company's officers, and disclosure of pending lawsuits.

proxy: An absentee ballot for shareholders to vote at an annual meeting.

public corporation: A corporation that offers ownership through the sale of stock to the public. Public corporations are required by law to disclose specific information about their financial condition and operations.

publicly held corporation: A company that sells stock to the general public.

quarter: Three months.

quote: A stock's trading price.

recession: The period in an economic cycle that exhibits a decline in spending and business activity.

recovery: The period in an economic cycle that exhibits an increase in business activity.

research and development (R&D): The process of investing retained earnings and capital for improving existing products and creating new ones.

resistance: A theoretical upper limit above which the price of a stock does not seem to rise.

retained earnings: Money a company receives from sales that it reinvests into the business before paying dividends.

revenues: Assets from dividends, interest, rent, and the sale of goods and services.

risk: The potential to experience a financial loss.

round lot: A block of 100 shares of stock.

Russell 2000: An index that measures the stock prices of 2,000 companies the average market capitalization of which is $288 million. These are considered small companies.

safety: A ranking that appears in *The Value Line Investment Survey* that measures the volatility of a stock's price. Scale: 1 (least volatile) to 5 (most volatile).

sales per employee: Net sales divided by number of employees.

seat: Membership on a stock exchange that enables the owner to trade without a broker.

sector: A market category.

securities: Investment instruments, including stocks and bonds.

Securities and Exchange Commission (SEC): The federal agency that regulates the sale of securities.

share: A unit of ownership in a company.

shareholder: An individual who owns stock in a company.

shareholders' equity: The value of preferred and common stock outstanding.

small-capitalization stock: The stock of a relatively small company.

speculation: A strategy by which an investor buys stock based on the potential for its price to rise.

split: A process by which the number of shares of outstanding stock in a particular company increases while the price of the stock decreases in order to make the stock price more attractive and broaden ownership.

spread: The difference between a stock's bid price and asking price.

Standard & Poor's 500 Stock Index (S&P 500): A measurement of the stock prices of 500 small-, mid-, and large-capitalization companies in a variety of sectors that uses a weighted calculating system whereby larger companies have more influence.

statement of cash flows: A report that includes information about a company's intake and outgo of cash over a period of time.

stock: A share of ownership in a company.

stock market: A place where shares of corporate ownership are bought and sold.

stock price stability: A rating that appears in *The Value Line Investment Survey* that measures a stock's volatility in relation to the market. Scale: 100 (most stable) to 5 (least).

Stock Selection Guide: An NAIC form designed to assist investors evaluate stock.

supply and demand: An economic principle that dictates that if there is a shortage of a commodity and great demand for it, the price of that commodity will rise.

support: A theoretical price below which a stock will not fall.

symbol: An abbreviation of a stock's name.

syndicate: A group of investment banks.

technical analysis: An investment strategy that studies the historical patterns of the price of a stock and attempts to predict its future.

ten-bagger: A stock the value of which increases tenfold.

10-K: A document required by the SEC that provides an annual detailed description of a company's financial situation.

10-Q: A document required by the SEC that provides a quarterly report of a company's financial condition.

timeliness: A ranking that appears in The *Value Line Investment Survey* that measures a stock's predicted price performance over the next year. Scale: 1 (most timely) to 5 (least).

tombstone: An advertisement that announces an initial public offering (IPO).

total assets: Current assets plus net property, plant, and equipment.

total liabilities: Current liabilities plus long-term debt.

trading: Buying and selling stocks.

trading volume: A measurement of the amount of trading of a stock or a stock market.

trough: The lowest point of an economic cycle.

undervalued stock: A stock the price of which is lower than expected according to its financial analysis.

underwriter: See investment banker.

unit value system: An investment club accounting method.

upside-downside ratio: A measurement of risk on NAIC forms calculated by dividing the projected high potential by its projected low.

value investing: A strategy that bases investment decisions on the value of a company.

Value Line Investment Survey: A report that ranks the stocks of 1,700 companies on the basis of industry ranking, timeliness, safety, and other measures. It also provides information about historical pricing, trading volume, as well as a stock analyst's evaluation. The new expanded edition follows another 1,800 companies.

venture capitalist: A person or company that purchases stock in typically small, new private un-
tried business ventures.

volatility: Price fluctuations of a stock.

volume: The number of shares traded of a stock.

Wilshire 5000 Index: An index that measures the
performance of all U.S. stocks.

yield: A figure calculated by dividing the dividend
amount by the current price and multiplying by
100.

Resources

Organizations
American Association of Individual Investors
625 N. Michigan Ave., Suite 1900
Chicago, IL 60611
(312) 280-0170
Website: http://www.aaii.org.com

American Stock Exchange
86 Trinity Pl.
New York, NY 10006
(212) 306-1000
Website: http://www.amex.com

Dow Jones
200 Liberty St.
New York, NY 10281
(212) 416-2000
Website: http://bis.dowjones.com

DRIP Investor
7412 Calumet Ave., Suite 200
Hammond, IN 46324
(800)711-7969
Website: www.dripinvestor.com

Dun & Bradstreet
899 Eaton Ave.
Bethlehem, PA 18025
(800) 234-3867
Website: http://www.dnb.com

Federal Trade Commission
600 Pennsylvania Ave. NW
Washington, D.C. 20580
(202) 326-2222
Website: http://www.ftc.gov

Internal Revenue Service
U.S. Department of the Treasury
1111 Constitution Ave. NW
Washington, D.C. 20224
(800) 829-1040
Website: http://www.irs.ustreas.gov

International Association for Financial Planning
5775 Glenridge Dr. NE, Suite B300
Atlanta, GA 30328
(800) 945-4237
Website: http://www.iafp.org

Investment Company Institute
1401 H St. NW
Washington, D.C. 20005
(202) 326-5800

Nasdaq
National Association of Securities Dealers
1735 K St. NW
Washington, D.C. 20006
(202) 496-2500
Websites: http://www.nasdaq.com
   http://www.nasdr.com

National Association of Investors Corp.
711 West Thirteen Mile Rd.
Madison Heights, MI 48071
(248) 583-6242
Website: http://www.better-investing.org.

National Center for Financial Education
P.O. Box 34070
San Diego, CA 92163
(619) 232-8811
Website: http://www.ncfe.org

National Fraud Information Center
P.O. 65868
Washington, D.C. 20035
(800) 876-7060
Website: http://www.fraud.org

New York Stock Exchange
11 Wall St.
New York, NY 10005
(212) 656-3000
Website: http://www.nyse.com

North American Securities Administrators
    Assocation
One Massachusetts Ave. NW, Suite 310
Washington, D.C. 20001
(202) 737-0900
Website: http://www.nasaa.org

Securities and Exchange Commission
Office of Investor Education & Assistance
450 Fifth St. NW
Washington, D.C. 20549
(202) 942-7040
Website: http://www.sec.gov

Temper of the Times
1010 Mamaroneck Ave.
Mamaroneck, NY 10543
(800)388-9993
Website: www.moneypaper.com

Books

*The Beardstown Ladies' Common-Sense Investment
    Guide*, The Beardstown Ladies' Investment Club
    (Hyperion, 1995).

Beating the Dow, Michael O'Higgins (HarperPerennial, 1992).

Beating the Street, Peter Lynch, with John Rothchild (Fireside, 1994).

Buying Stocks Without a Broker, Charles B. Carlson (McGraw-Hill, 1996).

Everyone's Money Book, Jordan Goodman (Dearborn Financial Publishing, 1997).

How the Stock Market Works, John M. Dalton, ed. (The New York Institute of Finance, 1993).

How to Buy Stocks the Smart Way, Stephen Littauer (Dearborn Financial Publishing, 1995).

How to Make Money in Stocks, William J. O'Neil (McGraw-Hill, 1995).

Making the Most of Your Money, Jane Bryant Quinn (Simon & Schuster, 1991).

The Midas Touch: The Strategies That Have Made Warren Buffett "America's Pre-Eminent Investor," John Train (Harper & Row, 1987).

The Motley Fool Investment Guide, David Gardner and Tom Gardner (Simon & Schuster, 1996).

Starting and Running a Profitable Investment Club, The Official Guide from the National Association of Investors Corporation, Thomas E. O'Hara and Kenneth S. Janke, Sr. (NAIC, 1996).

The 100 Best Stocks to Own in America, 5th Edition. Gene Walden (Dearborn Financial Publishing, 1997).

One Up on Wall Street, Peter Lynch, with John Rothchild. (Simon & Schuster, 1989).

Terry Savage Talks Money: The Common Sense Guide to Money Matters, Terry Savage (Harper-Perennial, 1991).

Wall Street Picks for 1997, Kirk Kazanjian (Dearborn Financial Publishing, 1997).

Periodicals

Bank Rate Monitor
P.O. Box 088888
North Palm Beach, FL 33408
(561) 627-7330
Website: http://www.bankrate.com

Barron's
84 Second Ave.
Chicopee, MA 01020
(800) 544-0422

BusinessWeek
1221 Avenue of the Americas
New York, NY 10020
(212) 512-2000
Website: http://www.businesweek.com

Financial World
P.O. Box 420235
11 Commerce Blvd.
Palm Coast, FL 32142
(800) 829-5916

Forbes
60 Fifth Ave.
New York, NY 10011
(212) 620-2200
Website: http://www.forbes.com

Fortune
Time and Life Building
Rockefeller Center
New York, NY 10020
(212) 522-1212

Hoover's Publications
1033 La Posada Dr., Suite 250
Austin, TX 78752
(512) 374-4500
Website: http://www.hoovers.com

Hulbert Financial Digest
316 Commerce St.
Alexandria, VA 22314
(703) 683-5905

Individual Investor
P.O. Box 37289
Boone, IA 50037
(800) 383-5901
Website: http://www.iionline.com

Institutional Investor
488 Madison Ave.
New York, NY 10022
(212) 224-3570

Investor's Business Daily
12655 Beatrice St.
Los Angeles, CA 90066
(800) 831-2525
Website: http://www.investors.com

Kiplinger's Personal Finance Magazine
1729 H St. NW
Washington, D.C. 20006
(202) 887-6400
Website: http://www.kiplinger.com

Money
P.O. Box 60001
Tampa, FL 33660
(800) 633-9970

Moody's Handbook of Common Stocks
99 Church St.
New York, NY 10007
(212) 553-0300

The New York Times
P.O. Box 2047
S. Hackensack, NJ 07606
(800) 631-2500

Pensions & Investments
965 E. Jefferson
Detroit, MI 48107
(800) 678-9595
Website: http://www.pionline.com

Smart Money
P.O. Box 7538
Red Oak, IA 51591
(800) 444-4204

Standard & Poor's Stock Reports
25 Broadway
New York, NY 10004
(212) 208-8000
Website: http://www.stockinfo.standardpoor.com

The Value Line Investment Survey
220 East 42nd St., 6th floor
New York, NY 10017
(212) 907-1500
Website: http://www.valueline.com

The Wall Street Journal
200 Liberty St.
New York, NY 10281
(212) 416-2000

Worth
P.O. Box 55420
Boulder, CO 80322
(800) 777-1851
Website: http://www.worth.com

Zacks Analyst Watch
155 N. Wacker Dr.
Chicago, IL 60606
(800) 399-6659

Index

The Beardstown Ladies are fourteen women who are members of an investment club that was established fifteen years ago. They live in or near Beardstown, Illinois, and still hold regular meetings on the first Thursday of every month. They are the authors of four best-selling books, *The Beardstown Ladies' Common-Sense Investment Guide*, *The Beardstown Ladies' Stitch-in-Time Guide to Growing Your Nest Egg*, *The Beardstown Ladies' Guide to Smart Spending for Big Savings*, and *The Beardstown Ladies Little Book of Investment Wisdom*.

Robin Dellabough is associate publisher at Seth Godin Productions. A former freelance writer, she has worked on more than a dozen books, including *The Beardstown Ladies' Stitch-in-Time Guide to Growing Your Nest Egg*, and *The Beardstown Ladies' Guide to Smart Spending for Big Savings*.

Seth Godin Productions creates books in Irvington-on-Hudson, New York. To date, it has more than 90 titles in print, including works on business, celebrities, computers, and more.